COLLEGIATE GOTHIC

COLLEGIATE GOTHIC

The Architecture of RHODES COLLEGE

William Morgan
With a Foreword by Helen Searing

University of Missouri Press

University of Missouri Press, Columbia, Missouri 65211
Printed and bound in Japan

Library of Congress Cataloging-in-Publication Data

Morgan, William, 1944-

Collegiate gothic : the architecture of Rhodes College /
William Morgan.
p. cm.
Bibliography: p.
ISBN 0-8262-0699-9 (alk. paper)
1. Rhodes College—Buildings. 2. Gothic revival
(Architecture)—Tennessee—Memphis. I. Title.
LD4707.M67 1989
378.768'19—dc20 89-4861
CIP

∞™ This paper meets the minimum requirements of
the American National Standard for Permanence of Paper
for Printed Library Materials, Z39.48, 1984.

In memory of
Charles E. Diehl and Minot C. Morgan
friends in faith

Contents

Foreword

by Helen Searing

The first critical and historical writings about American collegiate buildings began to circulate in the early years of the twentieth century, when it was recognized that campus architecture represented in microcosm the most significant contemporary currents in planning and design. In 1903 there appeared in *Outlook* a prescient piece on "Recent American College Architecture" by Columbia University professor A. D. F. Hamlin, which prompted an admiring editorial the same year in *The Nation* entitled "The College Beautiful." From July 1906 to December 1907, *The Brickbuilder* published several articles on the American campus by architect Alfred Morton Githens; these were followed by an extensive series of ten essays by the distinguished critic Montgomery Schuyler, printed in *The Architectural Record* from February 1909 to May 1912. In 1929, the first monograph on this increasingly important building type became available: *College Architecture in America,* written by Herbert C. Wise and Charles Z. Klauder, whose Philadelphia firm, as we learn in William Morgan's definitive study, had been retained in 1922 as advisory architects to Rhodes—at that time named Southwestern—College.

Since then, surveys such as the Baxter Art Gallery's *Caltech 1910–1950: An Urban Architecture for Southern California* (1983; its content broader than the title suggests) and Paul Venable Turner's *Campus: An American Planning Tradition* (1984), as well as monographs and articles on individual colleges and universities, have explored the vital role that college campuses—an American invention—have played in the development of architectural and pedagogical paradigms. *Collegiate Gothic: The Architecture of Rhodes College* is an authoritative contribution to this steadily growing genre of architectural history, which necessarily includes the exploration of changing American goals in higher education and thus should attract a broad audience interested in questions of philosophy and social history no less than aesthetics.

Although Joseph-Jacques Ramée's uncompleted plans for Union College in Schenectady of 1813 and Thomas Jefferson's scheme for the University of Virginia in Charlottesville, executed between 1817 and 1825, had established powerful models, the tradition of orderly, "academical villages" to house and embody American educational aspirations did not take hold immediately. During most of the nineteenth century, the majority of institutions started with one or two buildings, often indifferent in design and execution, and expanded haphazardly by gradual and fortuitous accretion. After the Civil War, when colleges—both privately and publicly funded—were founded at an unprecedentedly rapid pace, the shift to a more democratic and practical curriculum and the prevalence of the Picturesque point of view maintained the popularity of the casually organized campus composed of buildings in a variety of historical "styles."

By the end of the century, however, the desire for order had been reasserted, and colleges embarked on master plans featuring complexes of stylistically uniform buildings logically arranged in formal sequences. As Rhodes College demonstrates, this impetus shaped colleges in the South no less than in the North, Midwest, and West and survived changes in architectural as well as institutional priorities. Contemporaneously and on a larger scale, the same wish for harmonious and systematically arranged ensembles of buildings and spaces produced the City Beautiful movement.

Although after 1900 the disciplined campus plan became the rule, the architectural language through which the buildings manifested this order could vary. Georgian, Spanish Colonial, and Beaux Arts Classical vocabularies were evoked to dignify and beautify collegiate buildings whether their program was residential, administrative, educational, or recreational. But the most cherished designs for colleges were inspired by medieval architecture, especially the secular Gothic found at Oxford and Cambridge. Medieval styles had the proper associations with learning, and moreover were highly adaptable.

The acknowledged expert, Montgomery Schuyler, preferred Gothic for college buildings, for "the meaning and value, and the perennial utility of medieval architecture, is that it is not and never was an architecture of mere convention and training [but] was founded on the nature of things and not on conventional assumptions." He also praised the cloistral quality of traditional collegiate architecture. Schuyler urged the modern American architect to emulate the combination of "cloister and hearth" characteristic of the residential buildings of English universities, and he approvingly quoted Anthony Trollope's admonition to "let oriel windows grace a college." Had Schuyler, who died in 1914, been able to continue his investigations to encompass Rhodes College, we can speculate with some conviction that its campus in Memphis would have received his sincere approbation.

One of the major figures in resuscitating the Gothic in America and transforming it from the idiosyncratic High Victorian to the more supple Collegiate, or "Modern," Gothic was the English-born Henry Vaughan. William Morgan's book of 1983 on this important but hitherto-neglected figure makes Morgan the ideal author to explore the architecture of Rhodes College. In the present publication, Morgan has not only illuminated the roles of visionary officials like Charles Diehl and respected architects like Charles Klauder, but has again performed his exhumatory magic by recovering for the reader Henry Hibbs, a gifted specialist in collegiate design who until the writing of this manuscript was almost unknown.

Further, Mr. Morgan has taken a beautifully calibrated group of buildings, astonishingly coherent although designed and executed over a period of more than sixty years—from 1922 to 1986—and made them freshly visible to us. Modernist hostility to Collegiate Gothic had for a long time obscured the physical and expressive traits that made this style the favored one for educational buildings throughout America from the late 1880s until the triumph of European functionalism—dubbed by its American apologists "the International Style"—on the eve of the Second World War. When in 1939 Ludwig Mies van der Rohe was invited to design the new campus of the Illinois Institute of Technology (then the Armour Institute) in Chicago, the gauntlet was thrown down on the very doorstep of a major urban representative of the Collegiate Gothic style, the University of Chicago, which from 1892 to 1932 had demonstrated the viability of this mode of building for the American campus.

In her book *The Uses of Gothic: Planning and Building the Campus of the University of Chicago, 1892–1932* (1983), Jean Block observes:

> Architecture stands in such an intimate relationship to man's physical and spiritual life that comment about it is frequently laden with moral phrases. Gothic architecture was, for the first forty years of the University of Chicago's existence, considered ennobling, inspiring and uplifting. With the advent of a crusading modernism it was viewed as dishonest, deceptive

and irrelevant. . . . Now we can look at man's built environment with a detachment that enables us to see it in terms of its meaning to its creators and users and to place it in the context of its own time.

William Morgan has magisterially accomplished this placement for the Memphis institution, which has remained more faithful to the "Gothic Quest" than the University of Chicago. Morgan has had to confront the same changing evaluations of Collegiate Gothic but has not allowed them to hinder his evocative and penetrating analyses of the campus and architecture of Rhodes College. Further, his interpretation of form has taken him into the realm of meaning as it is generated by architectural composition, materials, and detail on the one hand, and the intentions of clients—administrators, educators, trustees, benefactors, and alumni—and architects on the other. His text not only illuminates the creation of one college and its campus, but also provides a key to understanding the larger social, philosophical, and architectural issues that are engaged by this major programmatic type, the American college campus. As A. D. F. Hamlin observed in 1903, collegiate architecture represents

the disposition of the American people to increase their financial investment in the higher education—an investment not only in buildings, which, taken alone, might mean mere luxury, but in all that for which the buildings stand, and to promote which they were built—science, literature, religion, and intellectual culture of every kind. The American scholar may well point to these edifices with pride, assured that a hundred years from now many of them will still be looked upon with admiration, as monuments of the intellectual and artistic enthusiasm of an age . . . .

Preface

In its almost one hundred and fifty year history, Rhodes College has had many names—Montgomery Masonic College, Masonic University of Tennessee, Stewart College, Southwestern Presbyterian University, Southwestern College of the Mississippi Valley, and Southwestern At Memphis. The Rhodes appellation is relatively recent (1984), and for most of the period under discussion the college was known simply as Southwestern. Thus, that name has been retained wherever appropriate.

This study is about architecture as idea, as image and symbol, about how a particular style was employed by several architects to create an environment that reflected certain educational and cultural aspirations. Floor plans and constructional diagrams are necessary for understanding how buildings work, but as that is not the purpose of this essay they have been used only occasionally. Similarly, there is a story to be told about the materials and methods of construction of the buildings at Rhodes, and someday that tribute will give credit to the several builders, masons, and contracting firms that turned the architects' drawings into reality.

One of the architectural historian's constant frustrations is the dearth of documentation, the lack of records that might enrich the story or simply provide needed facts. Unfortunately, papers and drawings get set aside, lost, or forgotten, or they simply decay. Nevertheless, most extant materials that relate to the building of Rhodes have been made available to me. The entire Rhodes community has been forthcoming and generous, and although it would take pages to thank everyone, the results of their handiwork are to be found within these pages. Especial thanks to Loyd Templeton of College Relations, to William Short and the staff of Burrow Library, and to President and Mrs. James Daughdrill. Also, to architect Metcalf Crump and Mary Parrent, widow of college architect H. Clinton Parrent. Sandy Hartz, of the President's Office at the University of Louisville, typed the manuscript. While I take responsibility for the book's contents, my wife Carolyn and my children Whitney, James, Joel, and Lindsay also played important roles in the preparation of this book.

1 To Be a Pilgrim

Thy stalwart towers of solid stone,
Thy vaulted arches strong,
Inspire our loyal hearts each one
To fight against the wrong.
Our lives reflect the beauty of
Thy stately cloister'd halls,
And characters grow genuine
That grow within thy walls.

—Alma Mater

Rhodes College possesses one of the most beautiful campuses in the United States. And it is one of the very few established American colleges that has faithfully maintained its original architectural program. The Collegiate Gothic style ordained for the new campus of Southwestern Presbyterian University at Memphis has been championed for more than six decades with a constancy nothing short of phenomenal.

The college's physical presence is a monumental and inescapable factor of its identity, for the school's history and philosophy are embodied in its architecture. The buildings that help define this special place also make Rhodes College an American masterpiece.

Like any great work of art, the Rhodes campus is worthy of and demands critical examination. Although only one historian's view of why Rhodes looks the way it does, this study is a natural extension of the justifiable pride that comes from having stewardship of such a noteworthy physical plant—and of the spirit of scholarly inquiry which these halls were built to shelter and nurture.

In the spring of 1987, Professor Robert Russell of the Art Department invited me to Rhodes College to give a lecture on the Collegiate Gothic style. Although familiar with campuses like Princeton, Yale, Wellesley, Bryn Mawr, and Michigan, as well as their Oxford and Cambridge antecedents, I did not know Rhodes. What I brought to Rhodes was of far less importance than what Rhodes gave me. Rhodes College was simply a revelation.

My reactions to Rhodes were similar to those of Robert A. M. Stern, the Postmodern architect and historian, who had visited the campus for the first time just a year before. In his public lecture he described Rhodes as

> a dream for someone like me beyond all expectations. The architect Charles Klauder who designed it in the twenties and has worked on other places like St. Paul's [School] and Yale which I know very well, never had the privilege of having his ideas carried out with such splendor and so consistently for fifty or more years, a dream any architect has and any architect of his talent deserves. And I think of all those people at Rhodes who have supported that vision, that dream . . . .

Had this well-known New York architect, popular interpreter of our designed past, and apologist for the best of American eclecticism seen Rhodes earlier, one feels sure that he would have included it in his book and television series, *Pride of Place: Building the American Dream*.

Telling the story of Rhodes College's architecture is, however, not merely a matter of offering praise or extolling the virtues of a lovely place that had the good fortune and taste to erect handsomely designed and well-constructed buildings. As delightful as the end result may be, the building of a college over more than half a century is a complicated story. As cultural artifact the college contains many layers of meaning, not all of which can be easily revealed. A college is both museum and living organism, so we must explore the various historical, philosophical, and visual components that contribute to the collective idea of campus, place, and school.

To begin, the fact that two architectural historians who are among Charles Klauder's admirers did not know of the Rhodes treasure speaks less of their Northern parochialism than it does of the role assigned the Collegiate Gothic style in recent architectural history. Men of Klauder's generation and the traditional aesthetic they espoused have been eclipsed by the Modern movement. The year of Southwestern's opening in Memphis, 1925, also saw the construction of a new "campus" for Walter Gropius's revolutionary design school in Dessau, Germany. The Bauhaus, which embraced the machine and rejected the past, was to have a profound influence on American architecture, for soon after the advent of Hitler, Gropius and other refugees like Bauhaus colleague Mies van der Rohe were designing and teaching in America. Thus, the International Style arrived on our shores in the 1930s and dominated architecture until the 1970s. This European philosophy was so pervasive that architects who worked in historical styles, whether Gothic or Classical, were gener-

2. Rhodes College.

ally either denigrated or ignored.

The factory-like International Style, with its flat roofs and glass walls, spawned by Gropius, Mies, and their followers, has recently been challenged by what we imprecisely call Postmodernism. Americans are rediscovering ornament, polychromy, and previous styles: classical columns are appearing on the facades of shopping centers, skyscrapers are being adorned with peaked roofs and brightly hued cladding, and even tract houses are sporting the verandahs, bargeboards, and color schemes of the once-scorned Victorian. Part of this looking backward includes the reevaluation and reappreciation of significant but forgotten architects.

Nevertheless, an increased respect for the architectural accomplishment of Rhodes College is not simply part of a trend, a flip-flop of fashion, or even the rediscovery of something we had not realized we had lost. Nor can we claim that by maintaining a consistent style throughout its Memphian history Rhodes has been a lonely leader of the avant-garde, foretelling a return to Gothic principles. Nor is the use of "1920s Campus Gothic" a throwback, a refusal to face the modern world—a sort of "lost cause" that touches the hearts of chivalrous Southerners.

The architecture of Rhodes is something of a conundrum, an architectural puzzle. My first exposure to Rhodes made me wonder whether I had entered some kind of architectural Brigadoon. I was surprised and impressed at how faithfully Rhodes had maintained the original commitment to the Collegiate Gothic style. Learning that East Hall was but a year or two old raised questions that a fifty-year hiatus might not have. Is a place as attractive and appealing as Rhodes merely a stage set, a theatrical unreality, an Anglophiliac fantasy, a happy accident—or the handmaiden and reflection of a noble academic heritage?

The Rhodes campus deserves an outsider's view on why it looks as it does and an attempt to interpret its meaning, although no stranger can be untouched by Rhodes's seductive physical setting. Yet, as I was to discover, it seems that I was not such a stranger to Rhodes after all. Charles Diehl, the man whose vision initiated the Rhodes we know today, and my grandfather were classmates at the Princeton Theological Seminary. Minot Morgan was awarded an honorary degree by the small Presbyterian college when it was still in Clarksville. Had he seen what his friend and fellow pilgrim created in Memphis, it would have seemed familiar ground indeed—just as Rhodes made this writer, sometime Princetonian and historian of the Gothic Revival, feel as though he, too, were coming home.

2 The Gothic Quest of Dr. Diehl

There is in this country much pseudo-Gothic architecture, a cheap imitation which may content the ignorant or the untrained, but which calls forth the contemptuous ire of the enlightened critic. This we propose to avoid. Genuineness is characteristic of the heart of this institution, and we wanted this note sounded everywhere, even in the construction of the physical plant. It was to be enduring, for we were building for generations to come. It was to be beautiful, for the aesthetic side of man's nature is important and a college of liberal culture dare not overlook it. It was to be genuine throughout, free from all substitutions and cheap, make-believe effects, for this college has a hatred of sham. It is a source of satisfaction to know that our architectural ideal has been realized, and that not even the most caustic and unfriendly critic can now or hereafter indulge in a smile of derision at our expense.

—Charles E. Diehl
"The Ideals of Southwestern"

The architecture of Rhodes College is the legacy of one man, Charles E. Diehl. When he assumed the presidency of Southwestern Presbyterian University at Clarksville, Tennessee, in 1917, it was failing, having never recovered from the ravages of the Civil War. At the time of his retirement in 1949, he had moved his institution to Memphis and transformed it into a liberal arts college of national reputation. Having successfully transplanted the small Bible school from the wilderness to an attractive wooded site in a regional metropolis, Diehl determined that the new Southwestern would be a living embodiment of the best traditions of Western art and religion.

Diehl's goal was absolutely clear from the outset. Writing only four months after the new campus opened in 1925, he set forth "The Ideals of Southwestern": "We did not seek merely the good but the best . . . . Here was the chance of a lifetime; a chance to set the standard of an institution for all time; a chance to go forth unhampered by past mistakes, architectural or other . . . . Our purpose was to launch an institution which would endure for centuries." In somewhat less lofty terms, what Diehl accomplished is a masterful intertwining of two contributions of European culture to America: the pragmatism, evangelism, and missionary spirit of Scotch-Irish Presbyterianism; and the Anglo-Catholic erudition of the medieval universities of Oxford and Cambridge.

3. Charles E. Diehl, c. 1929.

Charles Diehl had been pastor of the First Presbyterian Church in Southwestern's hometown of Clarksville for ten years when he was chosen to be the college's president, and both the town and the college had strong Presbyterian associations. Clarksville had been settled in the 1830s by Scotch-Irish from Virginia and the Carolinas, and one of their first accomplishments was the establishment of a male academy. This fledgling academic venture was in the tradition of the "log colleges"—those schools that Presbyterians had started a hundred years before and which, as they grew into Davidson and Allegheny and Knox and Wabash, carried the learning of Edinburgh, Glasgow, and Belfast to the far reaches of the American frontier. As Raymond Cooper remarked in his history of Southwestern, "It had long been the boast of the Presbyterian Church that among Presbyterians learning and religion go hand in hand."[1]

Allied with higher education though the Presbyterians were, there was little architectural reflection of this patrimony on the Clarksville campus, with the exception of "The Castle" (Fig. 4). Built in 1849–1850, "in the handsomest style of Elizabethan architecture it arrests the admiring attention of every passer-by, no matter were he from Rome, that city of St. Peter's."[2] This not unimposing brick pile was a rather typical example of the Castellated version of Gothic Revival popular on college campuses before the Civil War. Yet, except for the Castle and Stewart Hall (a brick schoolhouse with a Victorian tower built in 1878), the Clarksville campus was hardly the model "which would command the respect and quicken the pride of succeeding generations" that Charles Diehl set out in his "Ideals."

When the former Clarksville college opened in Memphis on 24 September 1925, it was only five years after the governing synods of Tennessee, Alabama, Mississippi, and Louisiana approved the plan to move. Nevertheless, Dr. Diehl was able to throw open the doors to a Gothic Revival campus that, though smaller, was the architectural equal of famous colleges of the day. The vision that made it possible for Diehl to create what he had in a few short

4. "The Castle," Clarksville, 1849–1850.

years and to chart its future was formed by the president's education at the oldest log college—the "Mother of Colleges" herself, Princeton. While he did not intend to make his college the Princeton of the South, it is impossible to underestimate the influence of Old Nassau on Dr. Diehl.

In a talk given in the autumn of 1949 to the Egyptians, a Memphis "intellectual" society, Dr. Diehl spoke about how Daniel Coit Gilman had shaped Johns Hopkins and how that Baltimore school "was the first real university in this country, measured by the standards of the British, French, and especially the German universities."[3] Diehl was a graduate of the Johns Hopkins class of 1896, but his further education at both the university and the Presbyterian seminary in Princeton was to have a far more profound effect on his leadership, particularly in his determination of the style of his new college and his choice of architects.

The young West Virginian arrived in Princeton in the fall of 1896 to begin a combined divinity degree at Princeton Theological Seminary and Master of Arts at what had been until then called the College of New Jersey. That premier Presbyterian college was celebrating its sesquicentennial year and was in the midst of a profound internal revolution.

One of Diehl's instructors at Princeton was Woodrow Wilson, the son of Dr. Joseph Wilson, a former professor of theology at Southwestern in Clarksville. As part of the 150th anniversary that culminated in the College of New Jersey's being renamed Princeton University, the young Wilson was sent to Europe to study British and German universities as possible prototypes for the reinvigorated and aspiring academy. American education was closer to the German model, and that had been followed at Johns Hopkins, but Wilson argued that for historical, cultural, and spiritual reasons the new Princeton should be fashioned along the lines of Oxford and Cambridge. (An Anglophile, Wilson wrote his wife from this tour that were it not for her, he would be content to stay in Oxford forever.)

The Princeton University that was emerging as Charles Diehl came to town had just decided to halt the practice of allowing donors to choose the site, the architect, and the style of buildings they gave. It was declared that henceforth all Princeton architecture would be in the Gothic style. Al-

5. Blair and Little Halls, Princeton University, Cope & Stewardson, 1897–1903.

6. Graduate College, Princeton University, Cram, Goodhue & Ferguson, 1911–1913.

though not without a certain polyglot charm, the Princeton campus was hitherto a collection of Georgian, Greek Revival, Richardsonian Romanesque, and Victorian Gothic. Now, it was to be shaped into a unified whole by the Philadelphia firm of Cope & Stewardson, architects who had attracted Princeton's attention by their Anglification of the campuses at Bryn Mawr and the University of Pennsylvania—Tudor gateways, Perpendicular tracery, and Jacobean towers, all delightfully and respectfully reminiscent of the collegiate valhalla that Wilson so admired in England. By 1902, when he had become the president of Princeton, Wilson was able to write, "By the very simple device of building our new buildings in the Tudor Gothic Style we seem to have added to Princeton the age of Oxford and Cambridge; we have added a thousand years to the history of Princeton."[4]

As a newly minted minister, Charles Diehl left Princeton in 1900 to serve two missionary churches in Kentucky, then the First Presbyterian Church in Greenville, Mississippi, and by 1907 the pastorate in Clarksville. By the time Diehl became president of Southwestern in 1917 and moved the college to Memphis eight years later, Princeton had built one of the grandest Collegiate Gothic ensembles anywhere—and as one Princeton wag remarked, bigger and better than Oxford. Diehl must have followed with interest the appointment of the nation's foremost Gothic polemicist, Ralph Adams Cram, as supervising architect of the university in 1906. Cram's hiring of such architects as Day & Klauder, not to mention the construction of Cram's own Graduate College (Fig. 6), surely did not escape Diehl's notice. (Ironically, it was Woodrow Wilson's dispute with his graduate dean over the placement of the Graduate School that led to his decision to leave campus politics and run for governor of New Jersey.)

Thus, it is hardly surprising that when Diehl came to build his own new college, he not only understood the relationship of architecture to academic reputation, but also that he should choose the style of his alma mater. "Having decided to build along collegiate Gothic lines because of the infinite variety and charm of that type of architecture, we sought to discover and ally with us the outstanding authority in this country on collegiate Gothic."[5] This was Charles Z. Klauder, a Philadelphia architect who had worked for Cope & Stewardson on the dormitories at Princeton and whose greatest work, Holder Hall, was created for Wilson's Oxford in America.

Diehl had also learned the lesson of Princeton wherein the grounds were considered almost as important as the buildings, insisting that the new Memphis campus have a minimum of one hundred acres. On that land Diehl was determined to fashion the most beautiful campus in the South, if not the entire United States.[6] He employed picturesque Princetonian planning based on the quadrangle, and he adopted Wilson's Oxford-inspired tutorial system, to say nothing of his program to secure Rhodes scholars for his faculty.

But Charles Diehl went beyond his mentor and his sources in insisting that no matter what his college would build, it would be the best, that the success of his venture depended upon unity and consistency. Because of Dr. Diehl's unyielding Gothic quest, long after similar medieval-inspired campuses of the 1920s abandoned their master plans and stylistic unity, Rhodes College remains a paradigm of the American collegiate dream.

3 Philadelphia, Pa., Princeton, N.J.

I hardly know which to admire more: the originality and suppleness with which the Gothic idea is treated or the miraculous manner in which, with all this originality, the quality of historical association is preserved.

—Ralph Adams Cram on the work of Charles Klauder

The small but handsome college which began a new life in Memphis when it welcomed students on 24 September 1925 was a testament to the Gothic vision of Charles Diehl. Nevertheless, Southwestern might have appeared to be just one of a bumper crop of new campuses that sprung up in America in the period between the Great War and the Great Depression. In the freewheeling, high-rolling 1920s, there seemed to be no end to the flow of dollars for the construction of quadrangles and towers. Elaborate reflections of Oxford and Cambridge rose at Princeton and Yale, at Michigan and Chicago, at West Point and Washington in St. Louis, at Pennsylvania and Wellesley. Some of these were entirely new campuses, like Southwestern and Duke, while others were merely an embracing of the Gothic style. And while this golden age of American college building did have its Georgian devotees—as recollections of Williamsburg and Jefferson's Virginia sprouted at Delaware, Sweet Briar, Harvard, and Diehl's own Johns Hopkins—the 1920s represented a triumph and the climax of the Gothic Revival, which had first appeared on American campuses a hundred years before.[1]

The Gothic Revival, as developed and practiced by architects like Charles Klauder, Ralph Adams Cram, Bertram Goodhue, and a host of other medievalists who came of age around the turn of the century, was what Cram called "Modern Gothic." Creative designers might have borrowed much of their architectural vocabulary from the Middle Ages, but they combined past styles with a spirit of utility that suited contemporary needs. The work of men such as Klauder might also be called "modern" in the sense that it was a sober and measured reaction to what they perceived as the excesses of High Victorian Gothic. College buildings of the post–Civil War period featured picturesque compositions borrowed from any of several past styles—often several in one building—and employed as many materials, colors, and dramatic effects as possible (one of the best examples of the Victorian Gothic is Memorial Hall at Harvard of 1866–1878 by Ware & Van Brunt, Fig. 7).

In the first half of the nineteenth century, there had been some attempts at an identifiably collegiate Gothic style with "Castellated" buildings such as that at Clarksville and those found on campuses like Virginia Military Institute, Knox College, and the University of the South at Sewanee, as well as at Harvard and Yale. But to the present century these modest structures with battlemented parapets seemed too much like illustrations from the pages of Sir Walter Scott's romantic novels, whereas a newly imperial nation demanded a more fitting image for its burgeoning colleges and universities. At the same time there was in England a movement to formulate an Anglicized and more scholarly Gothic—the revolt against High Victorian that would lead directly to the development of the Modern Gothic.

The leader of this group was George Frederick Bodley, architect of a number of chapels and buildings at both Oxford and Cambridge, and who for religious and nationalistic reasons had little regard for the bacon-striping, polychromy, and Italo-Byzantine sources of buildings by William Butterfield, G. E. Street, and other High Victorians. Bodley and his followers sought to chasten English architecture, particularly for churches and schools, and return it to that glorious moment in the Middle Ages when Gothic blossomed in England. A Bodley building, such as Queens' College Chapel, Cambridge, of 1890 (Fig. 8), was notable for its monochromatic brick, restrained skyline, and adherence to pure English Gothic sources.

It may seem far away in time and distance from Memphis in the early 1920s to speak of one English architect's crusade for a revivified Anglo-Gothic style, but it has a direct bearing in that Bodley sent one of his draftsmen to America in 1881 to carry his message to the antipodal shores of the Atlantic. And within a few years the Boston-based and socially well-connected Henry Vaughan created a stylistic revolution with the design of the chapel for St. Paul's School in Concord, New Hampshire (Fig. 9). Of this pioneer work, in the style of which the early Southwestern would

7. Memorial Hall, Harvard University, Ware & Van Brunt, 1866–1878.

8. Queens' College Chapel, Cambridge, Bodley & Garner, 1890–1891.

become such an exemplary exponent, the ubiquitous Cram said:

> In Henry Vaughan's St. Paul's School chapel we return from the dazzlingly personal to the reverently faithful, the thoughtful and scholarly spirit that varies from precedent only enough to give the work life and contemporaneousness . . . . It is in no respect archaeological, except in the sense that it is absolutely correct in detail . . . . It shows how close one can hold to medieval models and yet be thoroughly modern, thoroughly alive and real.[2]

In his other New England churches and school chapels (like that at Groton, another Gilded Age version of the English "public school"), his library and science building for Bowdoin College, or his recreation of Oxford's Magdalen tower at Christ Church, New Haven, Vaughan provided English models for patrons seeking to establish a certain cultural milieu. That a certain segment of American society was ready to embrace such a message—and that it had now been taken up by many architects—is shown by the choice of Bodley and Vaughan to design a "National Cathedral" for Washington, D.C., an English Gothic heretic in a neoclassical city, and ultimately the final resting place of that Princeton Anglophile, Woodrow Wilson.

The many admirers of Henry Vaughan, besides the movement's chief acolyte Cram, formed a growing cadre of architects who could design a proper Oxford cloister, Cambridge chapel, or Eton refectory to suit American tastes. Of these Gothicists, probably the most respected and sought-after campus designer in the country was Charles Z. Klauder.

The son of German immigrants, Klauder was born in 1872 in Philadelphia, a city that had long held a leading role in American architecture, and where at the turn of the century a fine group of talented designers was emerging. Klauder apprenticed with several local firms, including the Victorian Gothicist Theophilus Parsons Chandler and the suave and famous Horace Trumbauer (whose Modern Gothic campus at Duke would arise at the same time as Southwestern; he also did the Widener Library at Harvard in a grand "Imperial Georgian"). But more important was Klauder's time with Cope & Stewardson, the neo-Goths whose Tudor campus at Bryn Mawr, begun in the late 1880s, had attracted the attention of Princeton's trustees, and who thus were given the commission for the first group of buildings in Princeton's scheme for a trans-

9. Chapel of St. Peter and St. Paul, St. Paul's School, Concord, N.H., Henry Vaughan, 1886–1894.

10. Charles Klauder.

atlantic Oxbridge. Klauder's handsome renderings of Blair and Little dormitories struck exactly the right chord in the hearts—and presumably pocketbooks—of Princeton's Oxford-gazing alumni.[3]

Klauder switched to the office of Frank Miles Day & Brother in 1900, where his considerable talents were recognized almost immediately, and he became a mainstay of the firm's design department. By the time the younger man was taken into full partnership in 1912 the Day office had produced some outstanding collegiate work, including what may well be the Philadelphians' masterpiece, the Holder dormitory and dining complex at Princeton (Figs. 11 and 12).[4] The 140-foot tower, modeled loosely on the late-fifteenth-century crossing tower at Canterbury Cathedral, became an instant town and gown landmark, not so uncoincidentally bringing to mind the prospect of Magdalen College at the beginning of the Oxford High Street. It became a touchstone, a design source, a parent and a grandfather to any number of soaring towers by Klauder and others, including that planned for Palmer Hall, Southwestern's first structure.

By the time Charles Diehl began to search for an architect for his new campus

11. Holder Hall, Princeton University, Day & Klauder, 1910–1916.

12. Holder Tower, Drawing by Charles Klauder, 1908.

in Memphis, Charles Klauder was the obvious choice. Between Holder Hall—and more than a dozen additional buildings he would design for Princeton—and the opening of Southwestern in 1925, Klauder had done work for Cornell, Yale, Wellesley, Delaware, Colorado, Pennsylvania State, and countless other schools, including St. Paul's. Even without the undeniably strong Princeton connections, it is hardly any surprise that Klauder was the one man to whom Charles Diehl wanted to entrust his Gothic Zion. Unfortunately, the Philadelphia architect whose work Diehl had personally inspected at Wellesley, Rice, and Princeton, and whom the pastor-president called "the best architect available," was overbooked. (In 1929 Klauder, along with Herbert C. Wise—another graduate of the Cope & Stewardson office—became the authors of a well-received guide to campus planning entitled *College Architecture in America;* given how much in demand he was, one suspects that Klauder wrote the book to satisfy all those who desired his services but whom he could not oblige.)

In a letter to President Diehl dated 13 March 1922, the Day & Klauder office suggested a solution that seemed almost heaven-sent: the Philadelphia firm would serve as advisory architects, while Southwestern would retain Henry Hibbs, a Nashville designer who had trained with Klauder, as college architect. On the following day, Day & Klauder and Hibbs signed a memorandum of agreement regarding the design for Southwestern. This straightforward one-page document, initialed by Klauder, states:

Day & Klauder would undertake to advise with regards to the general layout, architectural style and mass of the proposed group of buildings and as the work progressed they would give Mr. Hibbs the benefit of their experience in similar undertakings both as regards plan and detail and further advise him in the use of materials . . . .

For their services Day & Klauder requested of Dr. Diehl a two thousand dollar retainer and one-half percent for advice "leading to the preparation of full preliminary drawings," and a further one-half percent if drawings reached the working state. This arrangement seemed satisfactory to everyone, and Klauder's falsely modest disclaimer that "this would not give you buildings which have my distinct personality in them" notwithstanding, the leading Collegiate Gothicist's strong imprint would indelibly mark the future Rhodes and help it achieve notable architectural distinction.

It is also revealing to note how long before the move from Clarksville Diehl was hard at work making sure that his architectural dream would become reality. Through his considerable force of personality and unswerving devotion to his concept, Charles Diehl was able to obtain the best principles of the nation's leading campus designer and have them applied by a local architect who, unlike his mentor, would not be as distracted and would also be closer to the scene of construction. Hibbs was chosen, according to Diehl, "because of his accessibility and experience in the South."[5] Diehl also bought a quarry in Bald Knob, Arkansas, to insure a steady supply of uniform stone for his college. Such a move typifies the Diehl genius, but it also expresses his desire that everything be absolutely first class. As he later recalled:

13. President Diehl and honorary degree recipients, Commencement 1932; Henry Hibbs is on the far right in the front row, with Charles Diehl on his right.

Because of the excellence of the Southwestern faculty, it would have been possible for the college to erect shabby and inadequate buildings here, but that would not have appealed to the citizens of Memphis and it would have been difficult for them to realize the kind of institution Southwestern was intended to be and actually was.[6]

The Southwestern that opened in the autumn of 1925 must have seemed a sort of "instant Oxford," but this was obviously not the case. As we know much of the story and character of Charles Diehl, as well as something of Charles Klauder by reputation, we should also defer to the memory of the least known of the triumvirate who created the new campus.

At the time of his death in 1949 at the age of sixty-seven, Henry C. Hibbs was one of the bulwarks of the architectural profession in Nashville, but his roots and the forces that shaped him and his work for Charles Diehl are to be found further north in Philadelphia. Born just across the Delaware in Camden, New Jersey, Henry Hibbs attended the University of Pennsylvania at the very time that a group of Philadelphia architects was emerging as an unofficial school of notable creative eclectics. Hibbs helped finance his architectural studies by working in the office of their leader, Frank Miles Day, whose chief designer was, of course, Charles Klauder.

After graduation from Penn in 1904, Hibbs worked in the office of Cope & Stewardson, then architects to Princeton. He then moved to New York (perhaps in an attempt to separate himself from the avowedly picturesque Philadelphia designers and gain exposure to other seemingly less-provincial styles) and worked for a number of architects, including George B. Post, perhaps best known for his skyscrapers and French classicism, although he did create a major Collegiate Gothic campus for the City College of New York during Hibbs's tenure in the office. Hibbs came to Nashville in 1914 as the on-site manager for the firm of Ludlow & Peabody, then building the new campus at George Peabody College for Teachers. He stayed in the Tennessee capital and opened his own practice in 1916.

Given his start with such noted campus planners as Frank Miles Day, Charles Klauder, and Cope & Stewardson, it might have been more surprising had Hibbs not devoted much of his career to collegiate design. In addition to the core of the campus at Southwestern, Hibbs designed a number of academic buildings at several church-related schools across the South, such as Davidson, Mary Baldwin, Hendrix College, and Galloway College, as well as Vanderbilt, the University of Tulsa, and—the school most similar to Southwestern architecturally—Scarritt College for Christian Workers in Nashville (Fig. 14). Despite an enviable record of accomplishment (he was awarded a gold medal in 1929 for his educational work), and no doubt due to his adherence to a style soon to become unfashionable, the literature on this important architect is limited to one laudatory article in the *Southern Architect and Building News* of September 1928. Of Scarritt and Southwestern, an editorial in that professional journal says:

> A more noble group of college buildings are yet to be erected in the South. With such work as this before us we are positive that Mr. Hibbs has contributed much to a more refined Amer-

14. Scarritt College for Christian Workers, Nashville, 1924.

ican Collegiate Architecture. There is truth and beauty, originality and a scholarly conception of correct collegiate architecture reflected in every detail of these buildings.[7]

In the accompanying article, "The Collegiate Architecture of Henry C. Hibbs," fellow architect Charles I. Barber wrote that Hibbs "is not tempted by the modern desire for the sensational." Furthermore, Barber singled out Hibbs's willingness to use modern construction methods to achieve his aims of "good architecture . . . logic and originality without the slightest striving to be different." Barber notes with highest praise Hibbs's choice of Klauder as mentor and critic and wondered "how Princeton can be equaled in so many respects with so much less money."

Henry Hibbs and "the building committee representing certain synods of the Presbyterian Church in the U.S." signed the standard AIA agreement between owner and architect on 2 June 1922. This document stated:

The architect shall prepare a block plan showing an Administration and Class Room Bldg., a Science Hall, two buildings for the Liberal Arts, a Library, a Chapel, an Auditorium, a Tower, a Residence for the President, a Residence for the Dean, two gymnasia, two groups of ten dormitories each with separate refectories and kitchens and an athletic field and stadium.

This plan obviously represented the ideal, what was longed for rather than what the college could then afford. Another clause in the agreement requires that "full working drawings and specifications shall be completed for the Administration Building, the Tower, one Liberal Arts Bldg., five dormitories of one group, and one refectory and kitchen, one Gymnasium, the Library, the Chapel, the Science Bldg., and the two residences." Remarkably, the administration building, a classroom building, two dormitories, and a dining hall were virtually completed slightly more than three years later.

The original campus plan (Fig. 15) was not followed exactly, as is often the case, but its spirit has been respected for the most part, and its chief features are worth reviewing.

The central aspect of the Hibbs-Klauder-Diehl plan is the enclosed courtyard, or quadrangle. Even though the tutorial system of instruction would not be introduced until 1931 (a method encouraged by the hiring of former Rhodes scholars, who by 1936 comprised 25 percent of the faculty, as many as any other school except Harvard),[8] the inspiration was clearly to divide the new campus into humane modules as at Oxford and Cambridge. And Diehl wanted to keep the dormitory units small—150 to 200 residents—in order to avoid "the barracks and factory plans where students are herded like cattle."[9]

The architecturally astute Diehl did not have to wait for Harvard's President Lowell

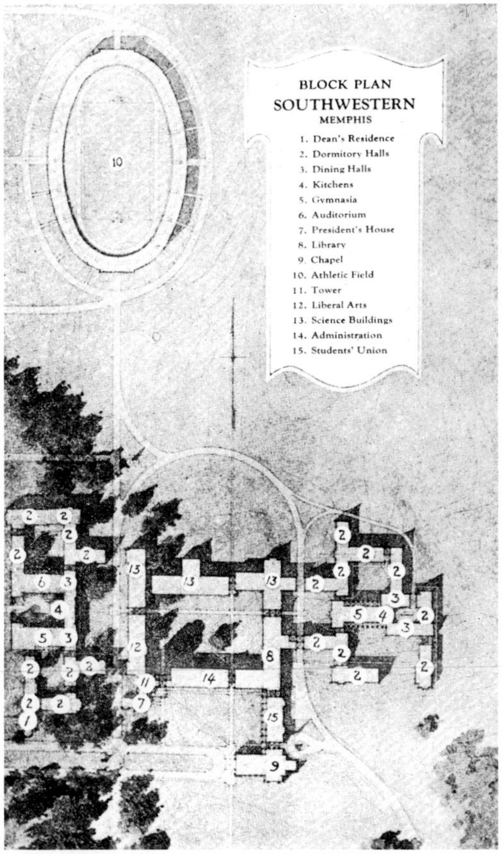

15. Southwestern, campus plan, c. 1923.

to introduce that university's "house" system in 1928, or for Yale to institute its "colleges" two years later, to appreciate the long-term value of the English college plan. For there were other reasons for Oxbridge cloisters besides aesthetic and spiritual longings. Diehl was consciously trying to plan for the future: "We realized that this college in Memphis could not remain small. Therefore, we sought in our planning to preserve the advantages of the small college, in spite of the fact that the numbers will increase, by adopting in large measure the Oxford plan of a cluster of small colleges."[10] From a practical standpoint, he and his architects understood the flexibility of a medieval plan that could grow at will without destroying the school's overall unity; unlike a rigid neoclassical plan that might have to be strictly adhered to, the organic character of Gothic is often improved with asymmetrical additions and accretions.

Charles Diehl also understood that there was little point in commissioning sensitive designers if you did not match their creativity with the finest materials and the best workmanship. Students, faculty, and intangible ideals might be the soul of a college, but the physical appearance of the campus could provide the "hard evidence" of the school's being. Most people know little about architecture or the nature of materials and therefore might take the looks of Southwestern for granted, but Charles Diehl sagely comprehended that appearances would register instinctively. Even if it meant constructing fewer buildings, these had to be the best: "We would rather do a limited work thoroughly and well than to attempt a larger work which we could not do in accordance with our ideal."[11]

It would stretch our admiration of Dr. Diehl to suggest that he foresaw the Depression coming. But he certainly showed foresight and prudence in securing the quarry in Bald Knob from which came Southwestern's characteristic warm brown sandstone. Today, college presidents are often chosen more for their business acumen than their scholarship, but it is amazing to think of the leader of a small Presbyterian college, a mild-mannered cleric with a pince-nez, with the prescience to buy the source of his school's building stone. Along with the masonry from across the Mississippi, Diehl prescribed Indiana limestone trim and Vermont slate roofs—materials that were not likely to be in short supply.

If Diehl's dreams of an Oxbridge along the Great River demanded a high initial price tag, his insistence on the best materials would pay back dividends many times over, not only as a constantly inspiring setting for learning, but also in terms of reduced maintenance costs. Charles Diehl refused to budge from his position that attempts to economize on architecture and construction would be foolhardy.[12] James Daughdrill, current holder of the president's baton, noted how Diehl held that "conviction through the Depression, and they didn't build cheap buildings then or now."[13]

As a result of this "build only the best" policy, Diehl could point out as early as the opening term of the new college that "the most beautiful college buildings in the South" cost less than the "same sort of buildings in those two colleges in the North."[14] What is so incredible is not that Diehl set his architectural standards at the level of Princeton and Yale, but that he was able to achieve those standards with an endowment in 1930 of only $438,960. "We were planning an institution," Diehl wrote, "which does not primarily concern itself with utilitarian values, but which contemplates a disciplined mind, a freed soul, a broadened personality, and an upright life."[15] Yet, his very attention to the utilitarian details allowed Diehl to create the nucleus of his dream within a decade of assuming the presidency of the struggling little college in the back of beyond.

When we look at Palmer Hall (Figs. 16–18), the initial building of the new Southwestern, we must again marvel at the guiding spirit of Charles Diehl—and at his choice of Henry Hibbs as architect. As the largest, most central edifice and the keystone of the quadrangle scheme, this administrative and academic structure had to be planned with care. Not only would it set the standard of subsequent construction in style, materials, and craftsmanship, but it could not help but automatically become the college hallmark—the equivalent of Princeton's Nassau Hall, Jefferson's Rotunda at the University of Virginia, or "Old Main" at scores of land grant colleges. In this respect the Diehl-Klauder-Hibbs team did not disappoint.

The first building at Southwestern was

16. Palmer Hall, 1923–1925, south front with entrance tower.

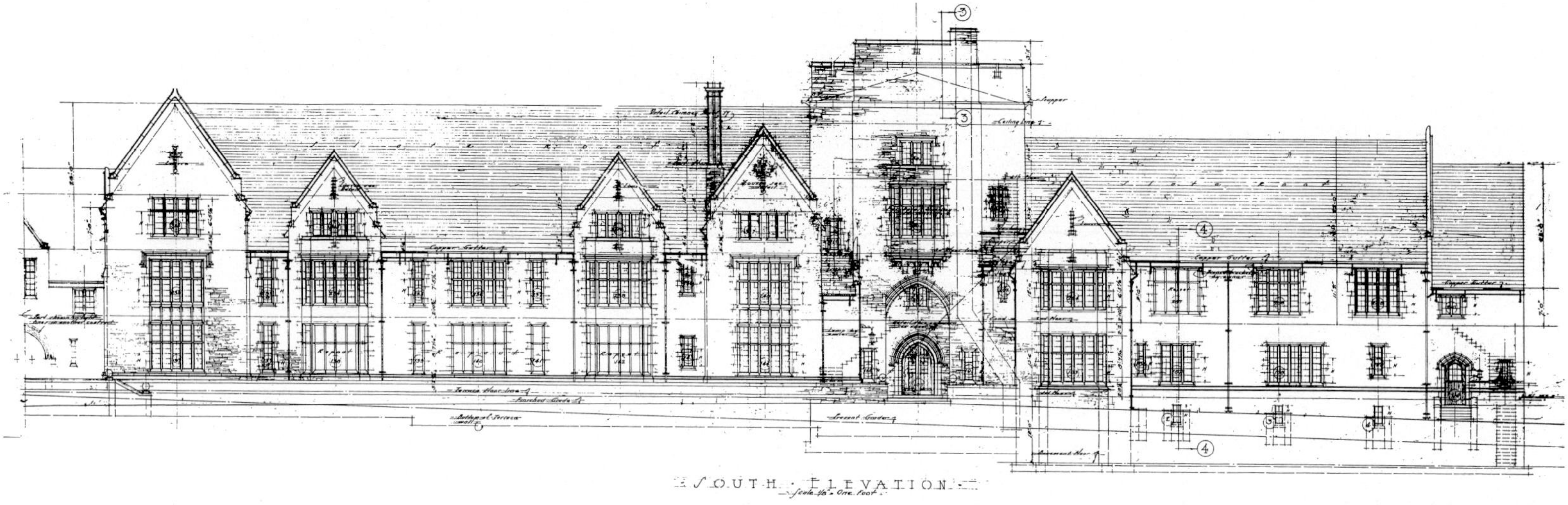

17. Palmer Hall, elevation drawing of the south front.

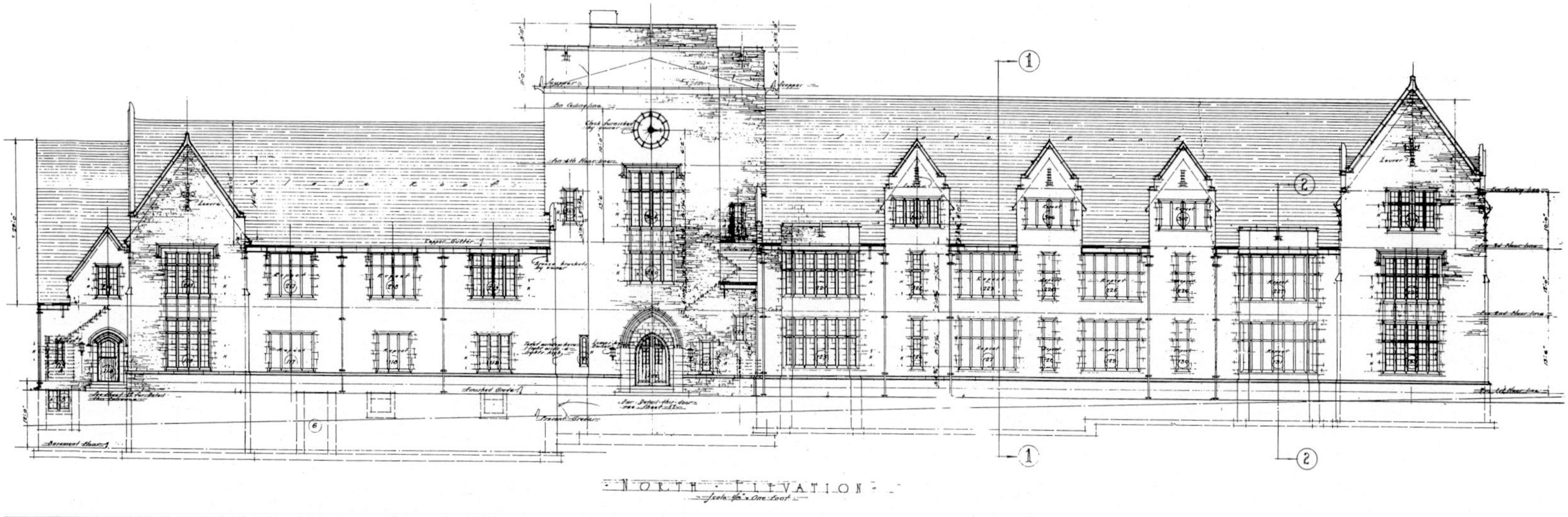

18. Palmer Hall, elevation drawing of the north front.

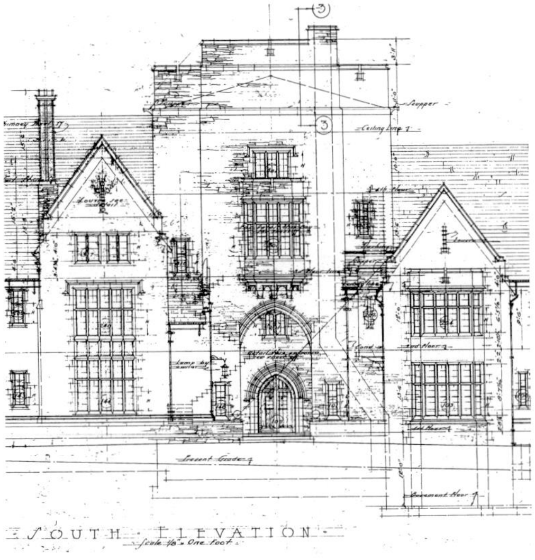

19. Palmer Hall, south elevation, detail.

named in honor of distinguished clergyman Benjamin Palmer, pastor of the First Presbyterian Church of New Orleans. As Dr. Diehl recalled, Dr. Palmer was not only "a great preacher" but also "the man who put the Louisiana lottery out of business."[16] Before he was tragically killed by a streetcar in 1902, he had worked hard to keep Southwestern Presbyterian University tied to the church, and he was both a good friend and trustee of the Clarksville college. Even a generation after his passing, Palmer's devoted friends and parishioners in New Orleans raised two hundred thousand dollars toward the construction of the building that would honor his memory.

Palmer Hall had to house a variety of functions: classrooms, the school library, and the main auditorium, as well as administrative offices. So even with the generosity of the citizens of New Orleans (whose gift paid for half of the building), it must have been obvious at the outset that the proposed tower planned for the west end of Palmer would be unaffordable for some years to come. Nevertheless, Hibbs and Klauder made Palmer suitably monumental by creating a slightly off-center gateway-cum-tower in the best Oxbridge-Princeton gatelodge tradition (as exemplified in St. Swithun's Quadrangle at Magdalen College, Oxford; see Fig. 20).

Framed by flanking full-height peaked gables, Palmer's blocky tower rises from a pointed-arch entrance. Above the archway is an oriel window that projects from broad masses of masonry. The parapeted tower appears solid, fortresslike, dominating, and yet this powerful image is purposely softened by the asymmetry of the flanking gables: one is three stories with flush fenestration, while the other has windows in only two stories but they project into a polygonal bay. Thus, the designer succeeded in establishing a picture of solidity, but with picturesque touches that lend visual interest and preclude an air of stolidity. The subtle rhythmic breaks of gable abound along the entire facade so that the composition is never static, never quite the same.

One need go no further than Princeton to find the sources for Palmer's re-creation of the spirit of the English medieval universities. The tower recalls Cram's Campbell Hall (1909), Zantziger, Borie & Medary's Henry Hall (1923), and, of course, the ever-inspirational Holder (Fig. 21). Palmer, a product of the same training, sensibility, and creative impulse, is not a copy of any of these, although similar massing, fenestration, and verticality is found at Klauder's Pyne Hall dormitory of 1922 (Fig. 22). The feature most reminiscent of Day & Klauder's Holder quadrangle is the so-called Cloister that forms the entrance hall of Palmer (Fig. 23). This square passageway composed of nine ribbed vaults, while not strictly speaking a cloister as in a medieval abbey or the recollection of Wells and Gloucester at Princeton, is nevertheless like a cloister wrapped around itself—a metaphorical cluster of chambers forming the heart of the Gothic campus yet to unfold.

Echoing the massing and general configuration of Palmer Hall—and of course employing the mellow Cotswold-like stone from the Arkansas quarry—is Science Hall (now Kennedy, Fig. 24).[17] Set at right angles to Palmer and acting as the northwestern anchor for the larger central quadrangle of the original campus plan, Kennedy, with its vaulted entry and its I-shape plan, has a north-south spine; its wings run east and west, figuratively pointing to

20. St Swithun's Quadrangle, Magdalen College, Oxford, 1880.

21. Holder Hall, Princeton University, gateway.

22. Pyne Hall, Princeton University, Charles Klauder, 1922.

dormitory quads off to either side of the main quad. The typically Klauderian vertical massing of windows and tall, narrow gables make the building seem more monumental than its two-and-a-half-story facade might imply, yet the scale is reassuringly domestic.

One might not always wish to seek out the architectural parents and ancestors of a Rhodes building, but it is especially interesting to note that Kennedy Hall predates two Klauder designs that it resembles, the Jones Mathematics Building at Princeton and Founders Hall at Wellesley (1931 and 1929, respectively). Furthermore, Kennedy's stepsisters are constructed of brick, thus supporting Diehl's contention that Southwestern could, by owning its own quarry, build more substantial buildings at the cost that other schools paid for brick.

There is not a curved line in the entire structure of Science-Kennedy except for

23. Palmer Hall, Cloister.

the arched doorways and the entranceway vaults. This verticality and angularity may have facilitated the housing of modern science equipment in a medieval-style building. And while one may be reminded of the scientific and scholastic legacy of the Middle Ages, what is more significant is that the architects created works of art that were indeed contemporary to the 1920s. With few decorative details, Palmer and Kennedy rely on massing and material to make reference to the past. But contained within the repeated verticals and the insistent linearity is a restless spirit that is just as much a reflection of the 1920s as the machine-inspired Art Deco or "moderne" buildings of the same time. Already these first two Southwestern buildings illustrate what Cram meant by the best Modern Gothic. Hibbs and Klauder endowed the college with sensible, functional, and contemporary buildings that are also reminders—not copies—of another age.

If Charles Diehl and his architects succeeded so brilliantly in the first academic structures, the president was even more determined to achieve the best with the residential group that would dominate the west half of the campus:

> . . . it is planned with the greatest care in accordance with our expressed ideal. The barracks or factory plan where students are herded like cattle is cheap, but it did not conform to our ideal. Nor, on the other hand did the plan of furnish-

24. Science Hall (Kennedy), 1925.

25. Robb Hall, 1925.

26. Calvin Hall (White), 1925.

ing luxurious suites with private baths or with lavatories in the rooms appeal to us as wise . . . . The dormitories were to be comfortable, sanitary, enduring and beautiful. They were to have about them the atmosphere of home. And thus there is nothing monumental about them. There is no suggestion of a horde or throng, but the domestic note is sounded, as distinguished from the institutional.[18]

Diehl's eagerness to provide "homes" for his residential college may account for the fact that both Robb and Calvin Halls (Figs. 25–26) were completed in the summer of 1925. (These first dorms were named after dorms at Clarksville; the original Robb was built on land donated to the college by trustee Lt. Col. Alfred Robb, who was killed at Fort Donelson; Calvin's name was changed in 1947 to honor Gordon White, a Nashville dentist.)[19]

When he referred to suites, Diehl was undoubtedly picturing Yale and Princeton, not least of all that fount for much Southwestern design, Holder Hall. As a compromise between hotel-like accommodations and long barracks halls, there are sitting rooms with attached bedrooms in the Oxford manner, and they open onto hallways that ingeniously make elbow bends halfway down their length (Fig. 27). Nevertheless, while Diehl might balk at a comparison of Southwestern's dorms with the suggestion of sybaritic residential living at his alma mater, there can be little doubt that once again Princeton provided the

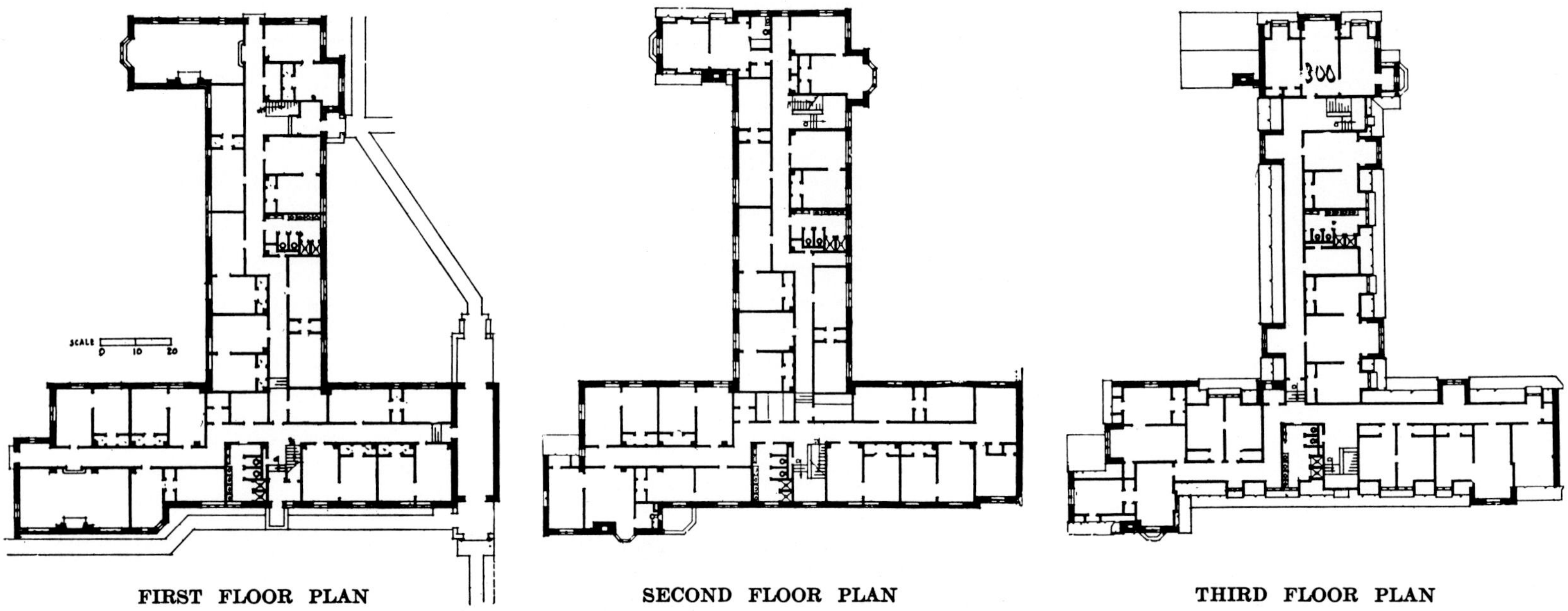

27. Robb and Calvin Halls, plan.

chief aesthetic inspiration (Fig. 28).

Robb and Calvin are indeed more domestic, less "streamlined" than Palmer and particularly Science-Kennedy; they are convincing evocations of the best of English academic villages, of the cloister and the hearth. Even though two single-block buildings cannot of themselves complete a quadrangle, every effort was made to insure a sense of enclosure by the use of projecting bays and minor extensions (like the social hall to the right of the main entrance of Robb). The rich pudding stone is capped by chunky slates of almost thatched-roof thickness. Dormers break through the eaves, and polygonal Jacobean chimney stacks perch on the roofs.

Given the fact that Klauder was involved in the design and construction of several dormitories at Princeton in the 1920s, as well as a number of academic buildings, strong similarities shared by Southwestern and its New Jersey counterpart were to be expected. One can even imagine Klauder and Hibbs, mentor and protégé, discussing the residential halls at both schools when the younger man went up to Philadelphia. The results at Southwestern comprise some of the most attractive American dormitories of the early twentieth century, and Robb and Calvin recall the Collegiate Gothic of Cope & Stewardson at their best, especially Blair and Little Halls at Princeton. In praising them Cram might have been describing Southwestern's new dorms:

> If there is anything more poetic, collegiate, racial and logical than the composition of these two buildings . . . so far at least as the product of the last four centuries is concerned, I do not know what it is. The thing is neither monastic or medieval, it is without affectation or theatrical quality. It strikes exactly the right note, it is sufficiently British, sufficiently American, a perfect model of sound design and impeccable theories.[20]

28. Cuyler Hall, Day & Klauder, Princeton University, 1912.

One of the pleasant aspects of Robb and Calvin is their social rooms, each approximately forty by twenty feet, each with paneled walls, low ceilings, fireplaces, and a genuine sense of collegial atmosphere. Notably, the floor of the Calvin-White social room is covered with tiles from the Moravian Tile Works of Henry Mercer in Doylestown, Pennsylvania. Mercer, who was an anthropologist at the University of Pennsylvania Museum during the time Hibbs was a student there, is best known as one of the leaders of the American equivalent to William Morris's Arts and Crafts revival in England. Similar to those employed at Bryn Mawr, Harvard, the Pennsylvania Capitol, and elsewhere, Southwestern's Mercer tiles suggest the level of sophistication to which

29. Neely Hall and Refectory, 1925.

the new Memphis campus aspired. Southwestern may have been in the "cultural boondocks" when compared to New Haven or Cambridge or Philadelphia, but Charles Diehl was determined that it would not suffer by its location.

Attached to the north flank of Calvin by a two-bay cloisterlike arcade is the dining hall, Neely Hall, also completed in the summer of 1925 (Fig. 29). Approximately half of the building's cost was contributed by Mrs. Hugh McDowell Neely as a memorial to her husband, a man Diehl remembered as a "heroic soldier and public spirited citizen."[21] Neely Hall extends the northward line of the main spine of Calvin-White, while it presents two large but quite different gables to the Kennedy-Science side. The eave of the smaller of these gables is broken by a single open belfry, which carries an 1848 bell brought from Clarksville. This, and the tall refectory windows divided by paired buttresses, give the dining hall an ecclesiastical atmosphere, yet Neely's domestic scale reinforces the air of welcoming intimacy established by Robb and White.

Inside, the twenty-eight by ninety-eight foot oak-beamed hall (Fig. 30) is an understated version of the college dining halls at Oxford and Cambridge, although its most immediate source is the one done by Hibbs for Scarritt College. The service wing at the northwest corner (now obscured by a recent expansion of the dining halls) was dubbed "the Kitchen of the Seven Gables" by Dr. Diehl. One especially flattering note—and one that must have been particularly gratifying to Diehl—was the inclusion of a plan and a photograph of Neely, accompanied by a glowing paragraph of text, in Jens Frederick Larson's *Architectural Planning of the American College* (1933).[22]

The smallest building on the new campus was the Harris Gate Lodge (Fig. 31), erected in 1926 as a memorial to Lt. Frank M. Harris, a sailor killed in World War I. Built as the home of "Mr. Johnny" Rollow, the college engineer, this one-story "house" has the same sandstone walls, limestone trim, slate roof (though here the ratio of roof to wall is well beyond 50 per cent), and bundled brick chimney stacks as at Robb. But the half-timbered entrance porch is one difference that makes this recollection of a late-nineteenth-century English cottage the most consciously eclectic of the half-dozen buildings that formed the fledgling Southwestern in the brave autumn of 1925.

There is one other important architectural feature of that new campus, the Ashner Memorial Gateway (Fig. 32). This monument consists of two lynxes bearing heraldic shields atop eleven-foot pillars (made of Arkansas sandstone and trimmed with Indiana limestone, naturally) in front of the south flank of Robb and to the west of Palmer. Charles Diehl understood the sym-

interesting—and revealing—genealogy. The lynx was chosen as the school mascot by Diehl in 1923, supposedly because of the creature's "uniqueness (and because a lynx is 'more pleasant than a skunk')."[23] It is unlikely, however, that Diehl never noticed—or did not actually have in mind—the pair of tigers holding shields that serve to decorate a gateway to Cope & Stewardson's dormitories at Princeton, and which the young graduate student must have passed hundreds of times. Surely they were also known to Henry Hibbs, who after all worked in the Cope & Stewardson office, and both Hibbs and Diehl undoubtedly had seen the tigers' leonine predecessors at Bryn Mawr (Fig. 33). Unique though it may be as a school mascot, the Southwestern lynx has a noble ancestry, a lineage that marks yet another reinforcing bond with Princeton.

Charles Diehl served almost another quarter of a century as president of Southwestern. He guided the school through a depression and a world war, but largely because of those two events he oversaw the construction of only two more buildings, both postwar dormitories. Although the name of his beloved school was later changed to honor another revered headmaster, architecturally he had seized that chance of a lifetime he outlined in "Ideals." He had built a small but noteworthy campus—the sturdy gate tower of Palmer and its cloister within, the domesticity of the dormitories, and the hundred-acre

30. Neely Refectory interior.

bolic importance of a formal entrance to the college, even if others might have seen such a nonutilitarian structure as a frivolous gesture.

With the exception of the shield on the gable end of Neely, these escutcheon-bearing felines are the only instances of overt symbols applied to the new buildings at Southwestern. Given the easily decorated and sculptural nature of Gothic, one can only wonder whether amidst the Anglican splendor of this little Oxford, Diehl preserved some spirit of Calvinist iconoclasm. Yet iconographically these lynxes have an

31. Harris Gate Lodge, 1926.

32. Ashner Gateway, 1925.

grounds were more than suitable starts on the Gothic quest. Equally important, he had created a blueprint for the future and had seen that it was followed, so that the present campus is Charles Diehl's legacy. His goals were spiritual and educational, but he knew that he needed good architecture to achieve them. A fitting tribute to the country parson who became a great builder would be to borrow the epigraph carved on the north portal of Sir Christopher Wren's St. Paul's Cathedral:

Lector, si monumentum requiris,
circumspice!

33. Bryn Mawr College, gateway lion.

4 The Colossus of Dr. Rhodes

You have today the unique distinction of standing in the midst of the realization of a dream, the solid substance of which you first put on paper and then clothed in rugged and beautiful Arkansas stone. You are at home here amid structures that you have nurtured from vague and halting requirements into forms of enduring beauty and usefulness. Possibly you alone can be said to have in complete and harmonious perspective the total concept of the design of this college.

—honorary degree citation
H. Clinton Parrent, Jr.

34. Lord and Lady Halifax at Southwestern, 5 April 1943.

35. 1944 Master Plan, pencil sketch by Clinton Parrent.

Charles Diehl's insistence on building only the best had served Southwestern well during the Depression; had he not built for the ages in the 1920s, there would have been no foundation for the campus plans of the 1940s and beyond. Small as the college was, Southwestern was able to join the war effort when it was selected as a training center for air cadets of the 13th College Training Detachment and the "ninety-day wonders" moved into Robb and Calvin Halls on 1 March 1943. A month later, Southwestern hosted the British ambassador to Washington, and a photograph of Lord and Lady Halifax standing in front of Palmer Hall, which was festooned with Old Glory and the Union Jack, adorned the cover of the college's financial appeal brochure of Janu-

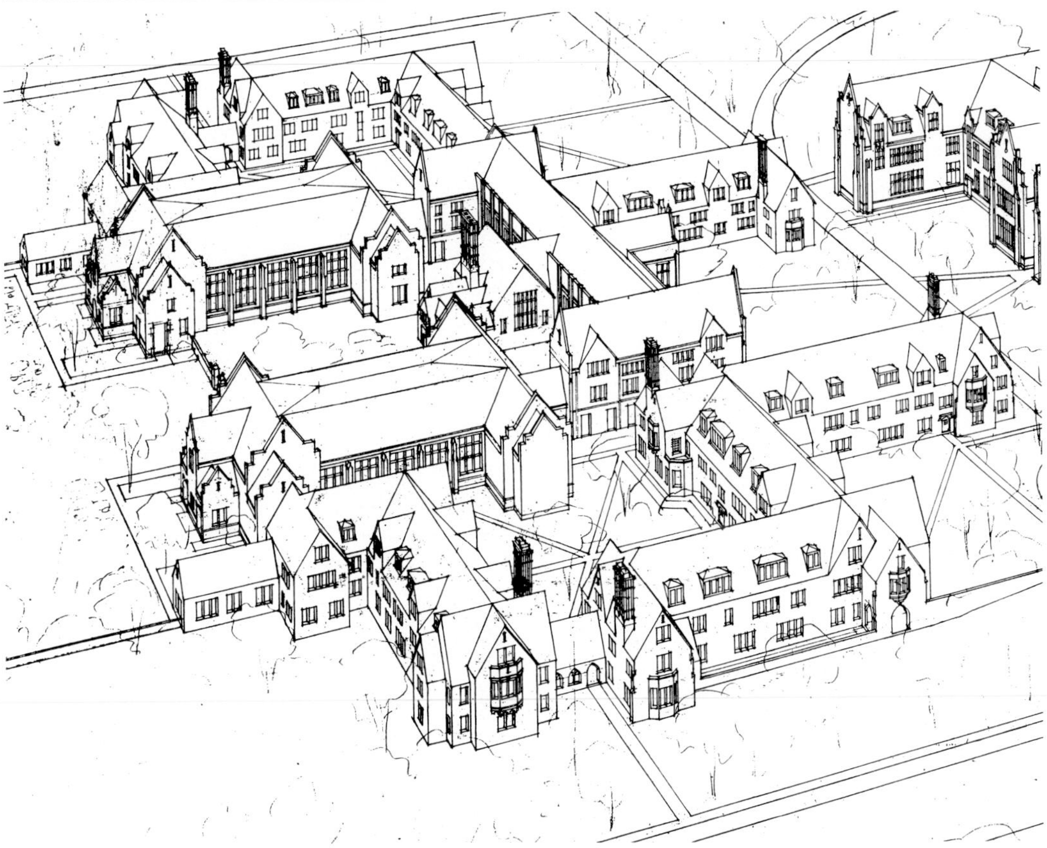

36. 1944 Plan, detail of men's dormitories-refectory-gymnasium.

ary 1944 (Fig. 34). The building that Diehl may have most regretted not being able to build in the opening construction burst of 1925 was a chapel. But in the two decades since he began the new campus, ivy and trees (including the oaks brought from Clarksville by Johnny Rollow) had softened Southwestern's aura of newness, and Dr. Diehl could be proud of "this little bit of England" that he showed off to his fellow defenders of Western civilization.

Nearly a thousand Southwesterners were fighting for democracy around the globe, and the appeal asked for "the money to keep on sharpening swords." Diehl, however, was also concerned about winning the peace, which could only be secured by "undergirding institutions of this character," and about continuing the Gothic dream for his school. In February 1944 the General Education Board of New York offered Southwestern half a million dollars if the school could raise an additional two million by December 1946. While 80 percent of the money would go into endowment, half a million dollars would go toward new buildings—a figure ten times the amount of the modest campaign initiated the month before. Anticipating both the success of the Allies and the generosity of the college's alumni and friends—and undoubtedly as an integral part of that appeal—Southwestern's architect Henry Hibbs drew up a new master plan.

"Southwestern, as it will appear when completed" (Figs. 35–38) was the realization of the several rectangles that formed the master plan of the early 1920s. Basically, Southwestern intended to complete the three sets of quadrangles: the men's dormitories, dining hall, and gymnasium to the west, women's dorms, gym, and refectory to the east, and the central academic-administrative quadrangle with Palmer forming its southern side. There are, however, minor rearrangements. The student center has moved north of the main classroom quad (where it was eventually built), and the

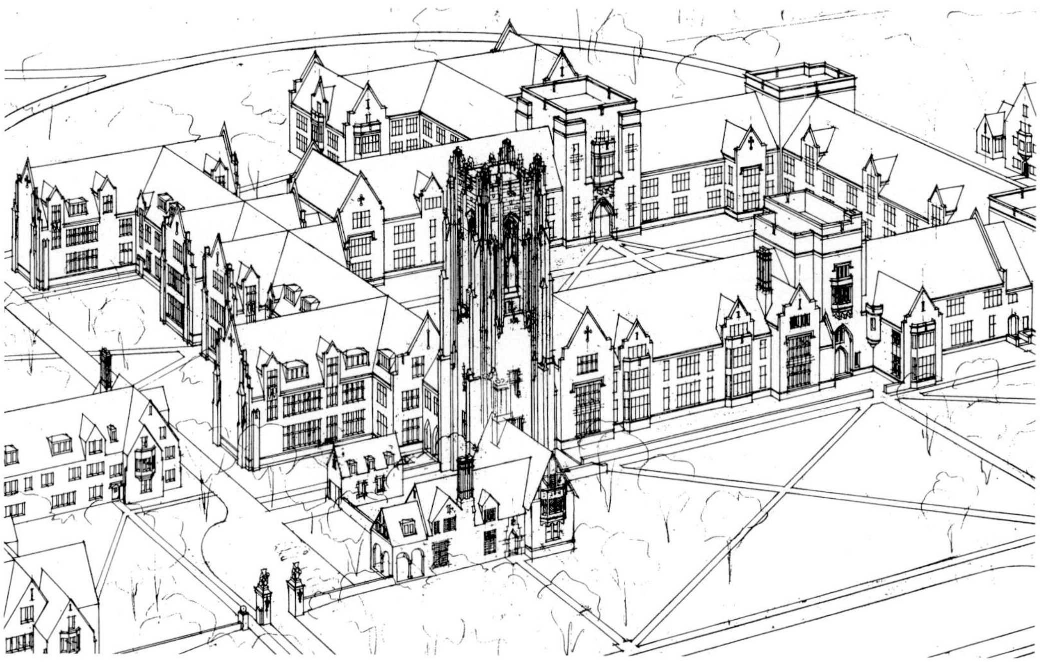

37. 1944 Plan, detail of administrative and academic quadrangle.

38. Proposed Memorial Tower, architect's rendering, 1944.

library has moved out of an eastern addition to Palmer to a space between Palmer and the chapel. The women's dormitories consist of a large H-plan block instead of smaller units forming an enclosed quadrangle as on the earlier plans, while the initially proposed Dean's Residence has been transformed into a President's House with a half-timbered gable and Jacobean chimney stack echoing those on the Harris Gate Lodge.

Nevertheless, the original Klauder-inspired vision of Oxbridge remains mostly intact. The buildings are generally long, narrow units with straight expanses of slate roof broken by intersecting gables, invariably near the end walls. A Memorial Tower (combining memories of Princeton, Yale, and Magdalen) stands guard over everything, but it is the smaller battlemented towers, along with the endlessly repeated small-scale units of multipaned windows, dormers, and domestically scaled bays, that bespeaks the spirit of the Anglo-Saxon collegiate model so beloved by Woodrow Wilson and a generation of Gothic Revival architects like Hibbs. Although these three particular towers and the north side of the nonresidential quadrangle were not built according to this plan, much of Dr. Diehl's dream was realized through the remarkable postwar building boom that more than quadrupled the number of buildings at Southwestern.

Two buildings went up during the last years of Charles Diehl's tenure, both of them dormitories designed by the Hibbs

39. Voorhies Hall, architect's rendering, 1944.

firm. The women's dorm had been planned since 1942, when Emma Denie Voorhies bequeathed funds for its construction (female students had been part of Southwestern since 1916). Before the war ended, Henry Hibbs's office produced a watercolor rendering of the proposed building as part of the college's money-raising efforts (Fig. 39). The overall shape of the building as constructed in 1946–1947 (Figs. 40–41) kept the basic configuration of long single block with a T wing fronting toward Palmer. One of the square towers envisioned in the administrative quad of the 1944 master plan was incarnated here as an entrance tower with felicitous results.

Much of the literature about Rhodes refers to the "consistency" of the campus, and while it is true that all the buildings use the same yellowish sandstone and New England slate, Voorhies shows how varied these Gothic compositions can be, even on one campus. The four-story central tower (whose parapet conceals a sunbathing deck) is flat and massive, and its relatively small window openings are limited to the upper floors. The tower's fortresslike appearance is somewhat mitigated by the civilizing openness expressed by the projecting oriel window at the second level. The tower itself projects slightly from the main block, and its verticality is reinforced by two flanking dormers. At the outer extremities of this facade are single story-and-a-half gabled projections, which frame the entire west composition. As these are repeated on the rear of this block, these elements give the impression of having been driven through the entire building.

Such subtleties may pass unnoticed by the untrained eye, but they were intended by the architects to give visual interest and to avoid sameness. The imaginative front of Voorhies is a far cry from historical pastiche and is a good demonstration of the depth of architectural talent that contributed to the creation of Southwestern.[1]

The 150-foot shaft of the Voorhies T running eastward behind the tower entrance is a pretty straightforward Princeton dormitory à la Charles Klauder: a long block whose walls are interrupted only infrequently by the occasional polygonal bay, with simple dormers hollowed out of the broad expanse of slate. Clearly, this long wing was envisioned as the closer of a women's quadrangle, as did in fact happen with the construction of Townsend and Trezevant a few years later.

The east wing of Voorhies did contain a special room, a small version of a building that Southwestern had always planned for and yet never erected: a chapel. Although

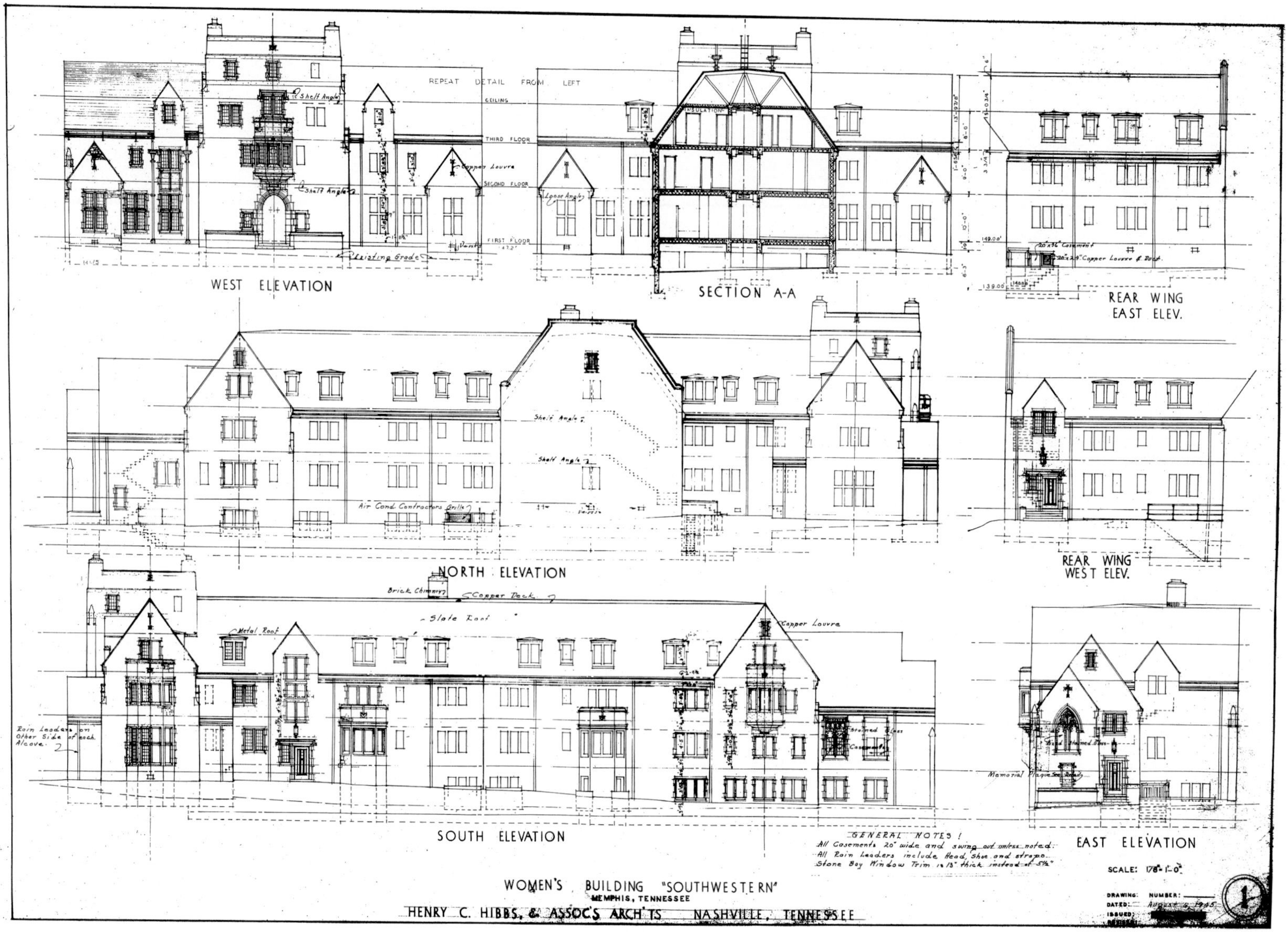

40. Voorhies Hall, elevation drawings, 6 August 1945.

41. Voorhies Hall, 1946–1947, west and south fronts.

only two bays plus chancel, the twenty- by twelve-foot Williams Prayer Room is another instance of the architects' creative abilities within what others might think restrictions of the Gothic style. The chapel, provided for by Miss Sallie P. Williams of Nashville before her death in 1939, consists of six pews, oak wainscoting, exposed rafters, and limestone-trimmed windows (Figs. 42–44).

It is the windows—a pair of double panels on the nave wall and a diptych east window over the altar—that set the mood of the prayer room. Created by Charles Connick, one of America's premier stained-glass artists, the rich blues and ruby reds of Mary and Martha above the altar and the figureless floral patterns of the nave windows form yet another link between Southwestern and the important figures in the Collegiate Gothic and the Arts and Crafts guilds which supported it. Since the founding of his firm in 1910, Connick and his chief patron Cram were largely responsible

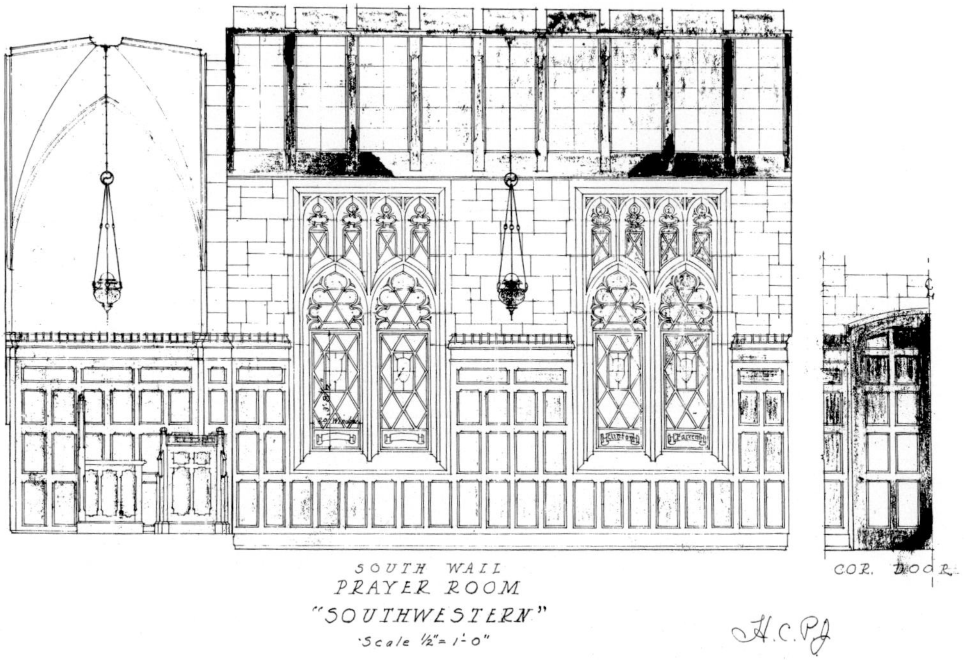

42. Voorhies Hall, Williams Prayer Room, south wall elevation, drawing by Clinton Parrent.

43. Williams Prayer Room, east wall elevation by Clinton Parrent.

for restoring the principles of medieval design to *stained* glass (as opposed to the Victorian fashion of treating the window as if it were a painting). *Adventures in Light and Color,* Connick's treatise on his ancient art, was published in 1937 and dedicated "To Ralph Adams Cram who trusts, encourages, and defends adventurers in Light and Color today."

Connick glass was often part of the glory of the major Gothic Revival buildings of early twentieth-century America. The Boston glaziers installed their art in Cram's partner Bertram Goodhue's University of Chicago Chapel, in the Cathedral of St. John the Divine in New York, and in Washington Cathedral, as well as the chapel at St. Paul's School. Connick's magnum opus is found in Cram's chapel for Princeton of the late 1920s. Connick's reflections in glass of Chartres and Lincoln in Cram's Princeton "cathedral" show how accepting American Presbyterians had become of the Anglo-Catholic forms of the Collegiate Gothic.

The Williams Prayer Room becomes understandable in these terms. Sheltered from the outside world, it conjures up the image of a private chapel from the days of Mary Tudor or Oliver Cromwell—an identification not inappropriate to a Southwestern that saw itself as a lineal descendant of the English medieval universities.

After the somewhat recusant atmosphere of the chapel and the fortified gateway of Voorhies, the other new dormitory built at the same time seems more restrained, more

44. Williams Prayer Room.

domestic. Named Edward Coleman Ellett Hall in 1956 in honor of an eye doctor and alumnus of the class of 1888, the "new men's dorm," as it was first called, had been planned as part of the original campus, and in fact its foundations had been laid in 1925. As an extension of Robb and Calvin-White Halls, it carries on their welcoming, humane spirit (Fig. 45). And Ellett continues the basic Southwestern building configuration of a long rectangular block framed by gabled wings (it is not quite an H or I in plan since it lacks a gable on the northwest corner, anticipating the future construction of Bellingrath Hall).

But there is more to Ellett than just its ferruginous sandstone walls, thirty-eight suites, social room, and assured best-of-Princeton manner. Some of the subtle tricks of wall articulation that we saw at Voorhies are repeated here. For example, the plane created by the walls of the south-side gables is also shared by the wall that connects them (and forms a courtyard which symbolically retains domestic privacy so close to the main entrance of the college). Visually, this plane does not remain static because the architect has created a feeling of movement by *projecting* a polygonal bay on the west gable, while the east gable has an arched *opening;* conversely, there is an oriel window above where there is flat wall on the west gable. By the simple device of indenting or projecting elements, the designers of Ellett created movement and rhythm against building masses that are otherwise planar, straight-lined, and rather severe. Except for the arched doorways, all of this movement and flow is achieved with nary a curved line—and without the expense of a lot of different skylines, curved additions, and sculptural ornament. Though ultimately based on medieval models, Voorhies and Ellett are not copies of anything: they are imaginative and individual, sensible and sensitive new solutions to age-old requirements.[2]

Three months before Charles Diehl ended his presidency of Southwestern,

45. Ellett Hall, 1946–1947.

Henry C. Hibbs died at age sixty-seven. This might have marked the end of an era for the design of the campus; however, Collegiate Gothic was too much a part of Southwestern's identity. Nevertheless, the usually prudent Dr. Diehl apparently did not anticipate the need for an architectural succession. Thus, when money was given for a library, the college turned to the firm of Jones & Furbringer, who had served as supervising architects from the beginning, chosen by President Diehl "because of their outstanding ability and their familiarity with local conditions."[3]

Voorhies Hall was the site of the announcement on 27 June 1950 of the largest gift made to the college up to that time—a six hundred thousand dollar grant from Mr. and Mrs. Aaron Knox Burrow to erect a library. In a typical rags-to-riches story, Mr. Burrow, the son of a poor Presbyterian minister from Macedonia, Tennessee, rose to become the nation's foremost merchant of cotton linters without benefit of education beyond high school. Dr. Diehl compared Mr. Burrow's gift to John D. Rockefeller's million-dollar gifts to Barnard and MIT and noted that the aims of both men were essentially the same: they believed "that first class privately controlled church-related colleges with high moral and intellectual standards are, under God, the bulwark of our future as a nation."[4] As the "Linters King" himself remarked, "I felt I should do something while I am living. This library will last. It's something that should be standing hundreds of years from now . . . . By helping the youngster, you're helping to build the future of this country."[5] Noble sentiments aside, Southwestern simply needed a library. As Mary Marsh, the college librarian, said, "We have become so cramped in our present quarters on the third floor of Palmer Hall that efficiency has been menaced."[6]

On the 1944 master plan, the library was to be sited immediately to the southeast of Palmer Hall and adjacent to Voorhies. As the munificence of the Burrows allowed a larger facility, the library designed by Walk C. Jones and his son, Walk C. Jones, Jr., was placed at the head of the main driveway, at the place where Diehl's chapel was originally envisioned (Fig. 46). Ground was broken on 5 January 1951, but because of delays caused by the Korean War, Burrow Library was not dedicated until October 1953. The final cost was just over a million dollars (the difference graciously made up by Mr. Burrow), and the result, as the *Commercial Appeal* had predicted in a 1 July 1950 editorial, was "a structure at once useful and lovely . . . . A splendid library placed in the hands of an institution dedicated to the teaching of manners and morals, ethics and religion along with the arts is a continuing benefaction."

Within months of the announcement of the Burrow gift, it was reported that the younger Walk Jones made "an inspection tour of outstanding library buildings in the east, including those of Princeton, Massachusetts Institute of Technology, and Harvard which are among the most modern and attractive in the country."[7] The reader cannot feign too much surprise in learning that, stylistically at least, the brand-new Firestone Library by O'Connor and Kilham at Charles Diehl's alma mater offered the most inspiration for Southwestern's new home for books. With holdings ten times larger than that planned for Burrow, Firestone is situated next to Cram's chapel, and the firm known primarily for their school and university libraries did a masterful job in putting much of the library underground and using terraces on the downhill slopes on the side away from the chapel (prompting Frank Lloyd Wright to describe Princeton's library as an example of "Pueblo Gothic"). The father and son Jones team did something similar with Burrow by placing the six tiers of stacks to the rear (where the ground does slope, albeit only slightly), along the spine of the plan's T (allowing for possible future expansion, when the shaft of the T could become the connector in an I plan).

Because of the consistency of materials and scale, Burrow might at first appear to be identical to the other buildings on campus. The new library does have the Pres-

46. Burrow Library, 1951–1953, rendering by Schell Lewis.

byterian Gothic characteristics of straight lines, little carving, and few curves, but there are slight differences. For one thing, the principle facade is neither a flat plane nor symmetrical: the larger north wing is not exactly opposite, nor does it balance the smaller south wing. While Burrow retains some Klauderian verticality, the most obvious difference is the rather elaborate (for Southwestern) limestone paneling adorning the façade. This and the double arches are very reminiscent of the entry at Firestone Library. To judge from the description in James Roper's official college history, the iconography was a welcome addition to the unornamented Gothic of the rest of the campus: "Culture lovers found the whole experience a kind of Gothic euphoria. There was a stone-patting glow in both faculty and students for some time to come, as they passed under the esoteric symbols of the seven liberal arts carved above the front loggia."[8] Beyond that loggia is an interior which, despite its warm oak paneling, is all businesslike efficiency—a prime example of what we might label "Eisenhower Gothic," and as good as that of the Princeton model.

The continuation of Diehl's Gothic dream was not automatic; there was in fact no architectural contingency plan in place at the time of Hibbs's unexpected death in 1949. But Diehl's successor, Peyton Nalle Rhodes, despite training as a scientist at Jefferson's neoclassical University of Virginia, was a great admirer of Gothic.

President Rhodes is perhaps best known for his filling up the campus with masonry. By the end of his sixteen years as president more than half of Dr. Diehl's fantasized forty buildings had become reality, some of them on a grander scale than envisioned. Construction became a way of life on campus between 1950 and 1970, with structures mushrooming by twos and threes, and dust, mud, and stone heaps being omnipresent as books and pens. Except for a three-year breathing spell, 1958–1960, just about every year saw dedication ceremonies for at least one new major structure.[9]

47. Peyton Nalle Rhodes.

And the logical man to carry on the design program of the college was clearly at hand in the person of Hibbs's associate, Henry Clinton Parrent, Jr., who had worked on Southwestern from its very beginnings in Memphis.

Clinton Parrent (Fig. 48) was a native of Nashville, where his father was in the hardware business, and was a graduate of the Peabody Demonstration School. Before entering Vanderbilt University as an engineering student in 1921, Parrent took a summer job as a draftsman for Henry Hibbs. Parrent left Vanderbilt after two years and, largely due to Hibbs's encouragement, went to the University of Pennsylvania, where he was awarded the BFA in architecture in 1927.

48. H. Clinton Parrent, Jr.

Upon his return to Nashville, Parrent assumed his place at the side of Henry Hibbs. From the outset, Hibbs depended a great deal on the younger man, and Parrent was involved in the design of such major commissions as Scarritt College, Davidson College in North Carolina, the libraries at the Universities of Tulsa and South Carolina, and a number of buildings at Vanderbilt, as well as the library at Fisk University in Nashville. Parrent became a

49. Tennessee State Library and Archives, Nashville, 1952.

member of the firm in 1932, but considering his growing role in the office, Parrent felt that he ought to be taken into full partnership; Hibbs hesitated, although he did elevate his assistant to "associate" in the early 1940s. When Hibbs died, Parrent established his own firm.[10]

As the head of his own office, Parrent continued his library work, designing the Tennessee State Library and Archives Building (Fig. 49) in Nashville and the public library in Bowling Green, Kentucky, and serving as consulting architect for the Texas Archives and Library Building in Austin. He also designed such Nashville landmarks as the Presbyterian Board of World Missions office and the Nashville Electric Service headquarters.[11] Almost more important was his role as a leader and spokesman for his profession. The engaging personality and concern for his fellows that often positioned him as the "front man" for the artist-as-difficult-genius Hibbs took Parrent to the presidency of the Tennessee Chapter of the American Institute of Architects (1950–1951), and subsequently to the head of the Tennessee Society of Architects (1954–1955). As his wife, Mary Parrent, remembers, her husband "worked all the time . . . . His only vacations were to AIA conventions."[12] Parrent had high blood pressure, undoubtedly exacerbated by the stress of being a workaholic, and, like Hibbs, he died suddenly of a heart attack.

Clinton Parrent talked often of traveling when he retired. Although he had not been to Europe, he was, like many architects of his generation and training, widely read and keenly interested in architectural history. Southwestern may have been his favorite work, but he was an able designer in other styles. An inventory of his office library in 1961 includes both the monograph on Cram's partner, Bertram Grosvenor Goodhue, and Philip Johnson's study of Mies van der Rohe; Parrent owned books on Williamsburg as well as *Domestic Architecture of England during the Tudor Period*.[13] Throughout his career Parrent was interested in restoration. In 1933 he made a study of William Strickland's Tennessee Capitol to ascertain "what would be necessary to restore it to its original beauty"; twenty years later he restored the state library in the capitol.[14]

Architectural history also provided an outlet for the overworked designer, as he occasionally presented papers about architectural figures to his church or one of the several social organizations to which he belonged. One of these concerned an early Nashville architect, Adolphus Heiman (1809–1862), and was read to the Tennessee Historical Society in 1953. In recounting the career of the Prussian immigrant stonecutter, Parrent included something of his own philosophy about architecture:

The architects of Heiman's and Strickland's time were concerned with designing in a known style and building for permanence. Today we like to use the term "functional" or "contemporary" to describe architectural styles; and the widespread use of glass such as in the United Nations Building in New York, and the use of wood cantilevers and sun shades as well as poor leaky concrete block walls, demonstrates how little effort is being made to construct buildings which will last a hundred years or more. . . . The proof of good construction is use over a long period of time, *even a hundred years or more* . . . . In the final analysis, it always seems to be this aesthetic criterion which determines the greatness of a building . . . . To expect great compositions from mediocre minds is to extract beauty from a vacuum.[15]

Clearly, the buildings that Parrent had worked on with Hibbs at Southwestern and that he would design there alone were based on principles of permanence, but they were also the product of an independent and creative mind.

50. Mallory Gymnasium, 1953–1954.

The first building that Parrent designed under his own name was the new gymnasium built in 1953–1954, replacing the college's temporary gym, which President Diehl noted had "remained temporary for more than twenty-five years."[16] The William Neely Mallory Memorial Gymnasium (Fig. 50) was named in honor of a Southwestern board member, sometime coach, and onetime treasurer of the college, as well as forty-one other alumni killed in World War II. "Memphis Bill" was the captain of the Yale All-American football team of 1933 and had returned to his hometown to become a businessman and civic leader; he served without pay as coach at Southwestern for a season and in 1935 was king of the Memphis Cotton Carnival. Shortly after Pearl Harbor, Mallory joined the Army Air Force, and his "Operation Mallory," which destroyed twenty-two bridges in the Po Valley in 1944, earned him the Legion of Merit. Major Mallory was posthumously awarded the Silver Star for his last mission in Italy in February 1945, from which he did not return.[17]

51. Townsend Hall, 1955, rendering by Schell Lewis.

The new gymnasium, constructed in less than eighteen months at a cost of a million dollars, contained all manner of athletic facilities. Its main floor could seat twelve hundred basketball fans, while the ground floor had the requisite locker rooms, offices, and classrooms, as well as two handball courts. Around the basketball court was a balcony that provided an additional eight hundred seats and fronted five more classrooms.[18]

"Muscle Manor" lacks the skyscraper-with-religious-overtones tower of John Russell Pope's "Cathedral of Sweat" at Yale, and one looks in vain for the football-playing gargoyles of Aymar Embury's recently constructed Dillon Gymnasium at Princeton. Nevertheless, the simple and dignified front of Southwestern's gym seems entirely appropriate to both the building's function and to the image of the college—a vigorous yet restrained muscular blockiness that reminds us of a Norman keep or perhaps a Scottish castle. The main front of Mallory is a variation of the west facade of Voorhies: a planar and symmetrical composition subtly framing a slightly projecting battlemented block.[19]

Mallory continued a pattern begun with Burrow Library of altering the 1944 master plan. In that scheme, the gymnasium was slated to be built west of the refectory and behind the men's dormitories. And while sports facilities, in part because they require so much room, tend to be banished

52. Proposed addition to east end of Palmer Hall, 1955, drawing by Clinton Parrent.

to the fringes of most college campuses (Mallory is on the site of the football field in the 1920s plan), this removal of such a major building to the edges tended to fracture the cohesive quadrangle system that had been Southwestern's goal for so long. While visual consistency was maintained by the use of the same building materials throughout, the erosion of the quadrangular plan was potentially quite destructive. Parrent's Richard C. Mays Memorial Gateway, built in 1958 on University Street, helped somewhat to tie together this corner of the campus. Still, Mallory's construction demonstrated that the tightly woven Diehl-Klauder-Hibbs plan was bound to be modified by economics and reality.[20]

Parrent's next creation for what college historian James Roper calls "the building binge of the mid-fifties" was the Margaret H. Townsend Residence Hall, which opened in 1955 (Fig. 51).[21] Unlike the gymnasium, this dormitory for seventy freshman coeds was envisioned in the 1944 plan and was designed as a natural extension to Voorhies. In fact, the shaft of Townsend's T is joined to that of Voorhies, so that together the two buildings form a single H plan. Parrent's entrance front for Townsend anchors the dormitory complex's north end, but it purposely does not compete with the Voorhies gateway tower. With the opening of Townsend for the fall term of 1955, Roper remarked, "All campus femininity was now collected into one sandstone seraglio where all was secure."

Also in 1955 Parrent designed a "Proposed Addition to East of the Administration Building" (Fig. 52), a forty- by fifty-foot tower that would have closed off the end of Palmer facing Voorhies. Had it been built, this three-story square tower would have formed a battlemented gateway with Voorhies. Its form was to reappear six years later in the tower for Bellingrath Hall.

Now that there was more housing for residential students, the "great hall" of Neely was growing increasingly inadequate, and consequently Parrent was asked to extend

53. Burrow Refectory, 1956–1957.

the college's dining facilities. Once again, let us rely on the prose of Professor Roper:

That same December's cold earth was attacked by the builder's unrelenting spade. As a finale to the five-year frenzy of building, a new dining hall began to rise. Mr. Burrow having provided a banquet hall for the studious mind, now turned his benevolence toward the more mundane kind of nourishment. He not only contributed most of the needed sum himself, but was instrumental in getting the remainder of the $245,000 cost.[22]

The Catherine Walters Burrow Refectory (Fig. 53) continued the Southwestern tradition of speedy construction (it was finished in the fall of 1957, the spade having been wielded only the winter before), and it showed Parrent's ability to expand and improve his mentor's earlier buildings. Like most of the Hibbs-Parrent buildings, Burrow Refectory features an entrance tower, which is just north of the old Clarksville belfry. Burrow maintains the same roof line of Neely, with the somewhat unfortunate result that the dining hall ceilings seem a little low. Nevertheless, while not an artistic threat to either Christ Church, Oxford, or Princeton's Holder Hall, the reassuringly domestic scale of Burrow's exterior offsets the shortcomings of the interior.

In the last Southwestern commission of the waning Eisenhower years, Parrent was able to recapture some of the quadrangular spirit of the original plans. Completed little more than a month after John Kennedy's election as president (and built at a cost just slightly less than that of its neighbor Voorhies), Suzanne Trezevant Hall (Fig. 54) fashioned a quad that had not been envisioned in either the 1920s or the 1940s. Called East Hall until 1967, when the retired president of Colgate-Palmolive gave one hundred thousand dollars in honor of his late wife, this women's dormitory was placed parallel to Townsend and at right angles to the chapel end of Voorhies. The basic I plan is like a mirror image of Townsend, with the slightly wider and more prominent entrance end at the south, close to the Williams Prayer Room. The gap between the newest and the oldest women's dorms was bridged by a gated stone wall. Beyond the gate lies a sheltered yard, a place of repose reminiscent of the private gardens of Oxford and Cambridge.

54. Trezevant Hall, rendering by Schell Lewis, 1959–1960.

The medieval ambiance of the women's complex is not the result of archaeologically correct Gothic details like turrets and gargoyles, but rather the product of a sense of unity promoted by the warm Arkansas sandstone, the slate roofs of equal height, and the absolutely right proportions of the building blocks and their fenestration.

The underlying rightness of the Parrent buildings is one of the reasons that the Rhodes campus remains so attractive, so pleasant, and so appealing. Aside from the references to our educational and religious patrimony, this Gothic is the work of an architect whose underlying principles transcended style, and who understood what made the best of past architecture speak to man's highest aspirations. In his lecture on Adolphus Heiman, Parrent listed the attributes of architectural beauty as unity, balance, proportion, scale, rhythm, design sequence, and climax.

These principles have not been limited to periods, styles, nor to any single fine art as they also apply to music, painting and sculpture . . . . Good architectural design may be produced

55. Bellingrath Hall, 1961.

intuitively, may flow from the designer's pencil; but the composition, if good, is subject to logical analysis . . . . Analysis will establish a module and will help give certain relations which are logical, necessary, and of such a character that they can be perceived by the eye and satisfy the reasoning of the mind.[23]

Thus, while most of us can appreciate the Rhodes campus without knowing exactly why the buildings are so pleasing, architects like Henry Hibbs and Clinton Parrent gave a great deal of thought to how members of college and visitors to the campus would respond to rhythmical patterns (such as the series of changing views as one walks through a building or across a courtyard) and a sense of sequence: "Architectural design resembles the principles of rhetoric in writing. The sequences within a building begin naturally at the entrance, and they should lead just as naturally to some definite end."[24] Proper scale, such as achieved at Southwestern, may be subtle, but the campus would not succeed as it does without it. "False scale," according to Parrent, "is always an offense against good manners in architecture . . . . A consideration of scale must occupy the architect's mind almost continuously during the process of design."[25] Here, in stone, is the probity—"that passion for honesty and that hatred for all sham"—that Dr. Diehl demanded of his college.

Just as Trezevant had formed the eastern boundary of campus, a men's dormitory dedicated just ten months after its female counterpart demarcated the western side of campus. Although the largest and most expensive dorm to date (106 men, $550,000), Bellingrath Hall (Fig. 55) was only slightly larger than the residence hall slated for this site on the 1944 master plan. Named in honor of Walter D. Bellingrath, one of the college's most generous supporters, the new dormitory formed a quadrangle along with Ellett and White Halls. At the building's north end, the castle motif that marks the entrances at Voorhies and Mallory is repeated, but in a stronger and more severe form.

As fortresslike as is the square tower—almost a modern shorthand of an Oxbridge college gate house—the real surprise of Bellingrath is the little prayer chapel at the building's northwest corner (Fig. 56). This three-bay oratory with its overall verticality and brick interior is far less traditionally

56. Bellingrath Hall, chapel.

Collegiate Gothic than the Williams Chapel in Voorhies. Its very flatness and linearity makes it less like the work of, say, Cram, than of some of Bodley's followers, like Ralph Lorimer or Ninian Comper. Even more than the other Southwestern chapel, the Bellingrath sanctuary approaches being a conceit, an unexpected expression of Anglo-Catholicism or even Jacobite secrecy hidden away in a somewhat dour Scottish Baronial school.

Extending the line of the inner campus side of the quadrangle formed by the men's dormitories, the college's new infirmary was placed north of Burrow Refectory. The Moore Moore Infirmary (Fig. 57) was made possible by the physician who not only helped bring Southwestern to Memphis, but who also served as the college's doctor from 1925 until 1946. While the building with the double-barreled name continues the basic college configuration of an I plan, Moore Moore is only one-and-a-half stories as opposed to the usual two plus attic. Adhering to the regular little-more-than-a-year construction schedule (1961–1962, although the preliminary designs were made shortly after Dr. Moore's death in 1957) and using the ubiquitous Arkansas sandstone and Vermont slate, the infirmary does, however, challenge Southwestern's straight-lines-everywhere practice by giving the barest hint of a slight bell cast to the roof on the side facing Burrow. It may not be quite as picturesque as the Harris Gate Lodge of thirty-five years before, but Moore Moore nonetheless has an appropriately domestic-nurturing air.

The one structure that had been the keystone of the Gothic quest of Dr. Diehl was a soaring tower—a Memorial Bell Tower, as it had been called from the beginning. Thus, almost forty years after Memphis's answer to Thomas Arnold of Rugby and his architects plotted the future shape of the new campus, Clinton Parrent got to design that most important of all structures, the one building whose aesthetics had to be immediately grasped by everyone, and the one that would become the visual symbol of the school (Figs. 58–59).

The location of the tower to the west of Palmer Hall had remained a constant, as did its basic form—a square, spireless English Perpendicular-style belfry of the Magdalen-Canterbury-Princeton type. As depicted in the 1944 drawing of "Southwestern as it will appear when completed," which Parrent himself had drawn (Fig. 37), the tower seems to be similar to James Gamble Rogers's recreation of Merton at Branford College, Yale. However, a watercolor of the tower (Fig. 38) that is probably from the same year reveals a flatter, more abstract, Bellingrath chapel-like composition than the more archaeological tower of the Vaughan-Cram-Modern Gothic manner. In other words, the linearity of the other campus buildings and their sources in the work of Charles Klauder (including his Cathedral of Learning skyscraper at the University of Pittsburgh) remain intact. Perhaps the closest source is the tower of Scarritt College in Nashville (Fig. 14). But the tower that has become, as it were, the trademark of Rhodes College was not, as we ought to know by now, simply a pastiche, but a creation that would be at once both traditional and contemporary.

As Parrent recounted in a paper presented to the Old Oak Club in Nashville in April 1963, he and Hibbs approached the design of the tower at Scarritt by selecting more than a hundred photographs of tow-

57. Moore Moore Infirmary, rendering by Schell Lewis, 1961–1962.

ers they admired. They then reduced the towers to the ten they liked the best and tried to analyze what common motif or module was inherent in the best designs. In his paper "To Build a Tower" (from which the subsequent quotes are taken), Parrent explained in detail how he reached the final form and shape of the Halliburton Tower at Southwestern. It was not just the result of intuition, but of careful analysis, much like the Greek approach to temple design, which revealed a rational and ordered basis for the "aesthetic criterion" that Parrent believed "determines the greatness of a building." Thus, the balance, the rhythm, the scale, the proportion, the sequence—all of what we have experienced in the previous Southwestern buildings—were studied in the process of designing the tower.

Simply stated, the form of Southwestern's dominating tower was the result of the architect's search for a module based on the human being, ideally a Golden Section. The arithmetical progression that Hibbs and Parrent worked out for Scarritt was 9:6:4, a sequence which they felt gave that tower "a feeling of being alive." For the tower at Memphis, Parrent refined this ratio to 10:6:4 (the so-called Fibonacci progression, named for a thirteenth-century Italian mathematician) and used the height of a man for the last step in the series. In the diagrams that Parrent used to illustrate his paper, he compared the Fibonacci scheme to the branches of a tree—and the architect refined the top of the tower so that it would be basically a heavenward-aspiring parabola. (The Fibonacci series was employed around 1950 by the great Swiss-French architect Le Corbusier in developing his own system of dimensions derived from the human form and the Golden Section; while not an admirer of Le Corbusier's brightly colored and sculptural buildings of rough concrete, Parrent was no doubt familiar with the "Modulor.")

Parrent's seventeen-page typescript also gives a variety of statistics about the tower's weight, footing, and construction, as well as praise for the contractors (Canfield & Scarborough) and the integrity of the masons, and a description of how they together came up with stained Indiana limestone on the tower to match the "Nashville travertine" of Palmer, which was no longer available. Most revealing is the designer's understanding of the importance of the campus plan and how carefully he and his mentor had tried to shape the spaces that held their buildings:

Formal and informal sequences produce completely different effects. The impression produced by the formal sequence is one of dignity, of directness and of definite and stressed climax. An informal sequence that was fixed for us by the overall design of the campus is full of the sense of dynamic and varied motion. Informal sequences may have units which yield an element of surprise and lead to the effects of apparently unpremeditated charm; thus they are naturally more personal in effect than are formal sequences. There is in them, usually, nothing of the awe-inspiring feeling that sometimes accompanies formal planning; they seem natural and human.

58. Halliburton Tower, 1961–1962.

Compare the above quote with that made by the tower's donor, Wesley Halliburton, at the ground-breaking ceremonies in 1961:

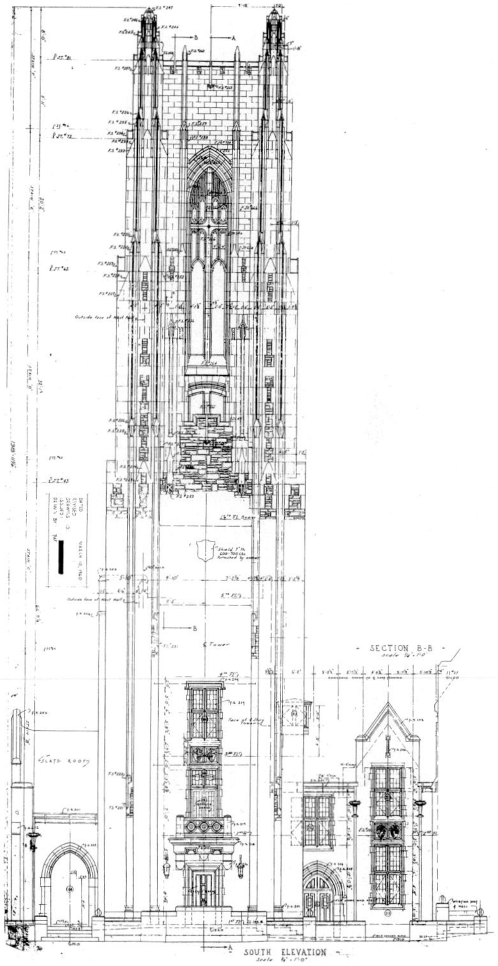

59. Halliburton Tower, elevation drawing by Clinton Parrent.

It takes more than four walls and a log to sit on to make a school house now. We must have BEAUTY in our schools and colleges, as well as protecting walls. But as of today, Southwestern is like a charming lady who is becomingly attired, lacking only a hat. Mrs. Halliburton and I decided to buy this lady the hat to complete her sartorial elegance.

60. President Rhodes and Honorary Degree recipients, Commencement 1958; Wesley Halliburton at far left, Clinton Parrent second from left, A. K. Burrow fourth from the left, and Peyton Rhodes to the right of Burrow.

At that time the patron was over ninety and had been a friend of the college since he had been instrumental in bringing Southwestern from Clarksville. The Vanderbilt- and MIT-trained engineer had gone into real estate in 1900, but had gained a certain measure of fame as the father of the world traveler and adventure writer Richard Halliburton. As Parrent recalled, the younger Halliburton's name was "synonymous with courage-action-drama and with the romance of faraway places, as one best seller followed another from his roving fountain pen, and the world's newspapers chronicled his exploits for a waiting public." When Halliburton was lost at sea in 1939 while trying to sail a junk across the Pacific from China, his estate went to his alma mater at Princeton, but his parents wished to create a memorial to Richard as a "Memphis Boy." So the tower was built in tribute to the author of *The Royal Road to Romance,* and the first floor of the tower displays Halliburton memorabilia.

Patron and architect met when both were awarded honorary degrees by Southwestern in 1958 (Fig. 60), and when they returned to build the tower, Wesley Halliburton took an active interest in its construction. Mr. Halliburton rode the hoists and observed the workmen firsthand, and, as he did not like carillons, he specified the single four-ton Bourdon that was placed 140 feet above the campus.[26] At the dedication on 17 October 1962, President Rhodes referred to the Halliburton Tower as "a sermon in soaring stone." An even finer tribute to the architect came from Wesley Halliburton himself.

And now, in the gratefulness of my heart, I must hope that you will have other towers to build, but I must express a doubt that you will ever build one more consistently beautiful than the Richard Halliburton Memorial Tower at Southwestern at Memphis. It is not the size nor material that makes for beauty, but the inspiration that comes from the soul of the one who plans it.[27]

That Southwestern At Memphis would someday build a tower was accepted from the beginning. But during the design and construction of Halliburton, Clint Parrent was designing a project which, if had it been built, according to President Rhodes, "there would have been nothing like it."[28] A nonresidential center for continuing education had long been a dream of Dr. Rhodes, and he wanted the center to be "a dramatic architectural form to express a dynamic urban educational concept"—a manifestation of "the discovery of the civic purpose" of Southwestern.

In 1957 President Rhodes approached the Kellogg Foundation to seek their support for a building or building complex that would "relate college and community by means of civic dialogue." The foundation had funded similar residential centers at a number of public universities, and "encouraged by the very cordial response," Southwestern went against its long-established policy of commissioning new architecture only when it had the funding in hand. "In 1960 or early 1961" Parrent was asked to design the Kellogg Center for Continuing Education, a project expected to cost about a million dollars. As Rhodes remembered, the architect "spent a total of two to three years" refining and elaborating the concept and had, in fact, just finished yet another revision in November 1963 when the Kellogg Foundation unexpectedly and inexplicably informed Dr. Rhodes that it could not "provide financial assistance for the excellent plan which you and your colleagues have developed for Southwestern."[29] Despite the disappointment at campus, and the unfortunate resentment that arose because of the college's inability to cover the architect's expenses,[30] the imaginative designs for the Kellogg Center are an important part of Rhodes College's architectural history.

The Kellogg Center went through a variety of changes in its three-year design history, but the site for this unusual medieval-yet-modern piece of architecture was fixed by Dr. Rhodes at "the east end of the E-W axis closed by the Mallory Gymnasium on the west." Had it been built in any of its various stages, its very size alone would have anchored the northeast corner of the campus.

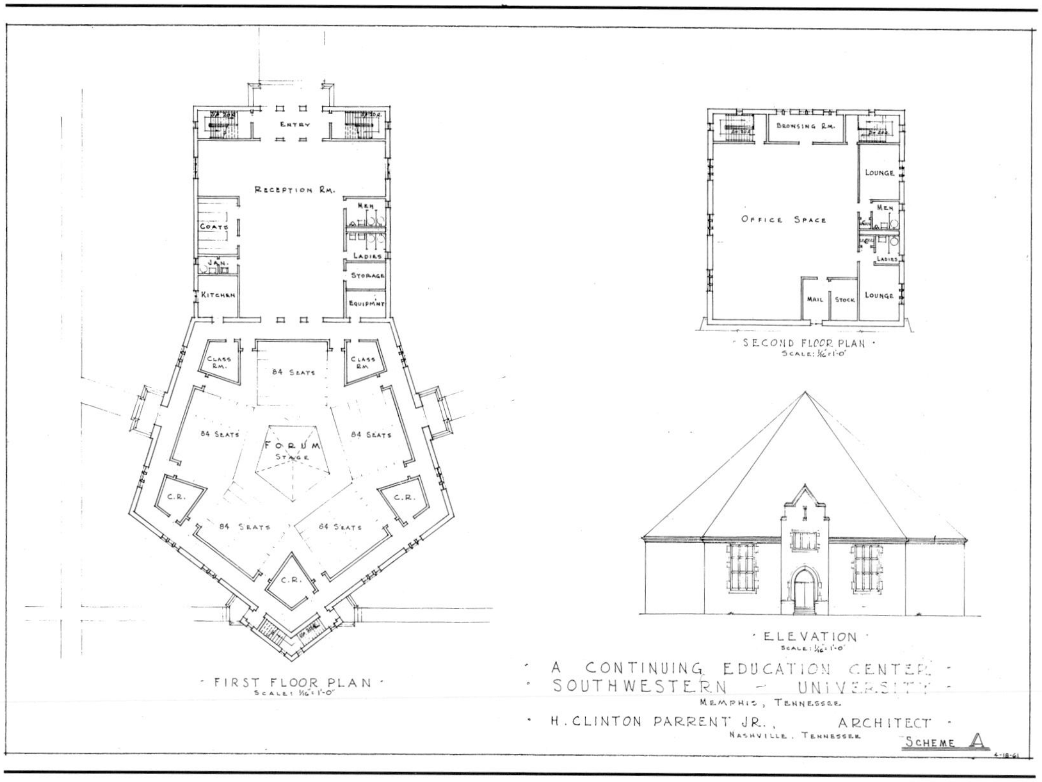

61. Kellogg Center for Continuing Education, Scheme A, 18 April 1961.

The first plan ("Scheme A," a pencil plan and elevation dated 18 April 1961, Fig. 61) was for a single pentagonal building with a square ell projecting from one side. The main block consisted of a large auditorium with five groupings of eighty-four seats facing a central stage called the Forum; five small classrooms were to be wedged into the outer corners. The entranceway on the square reception block was like the standard entrances seen so often before, but the whole would be under a dramatically peaked roof, giving the composition the appearance of an English cathedral's chapter house or recalling the abbot's kitchen at Glastonbury.

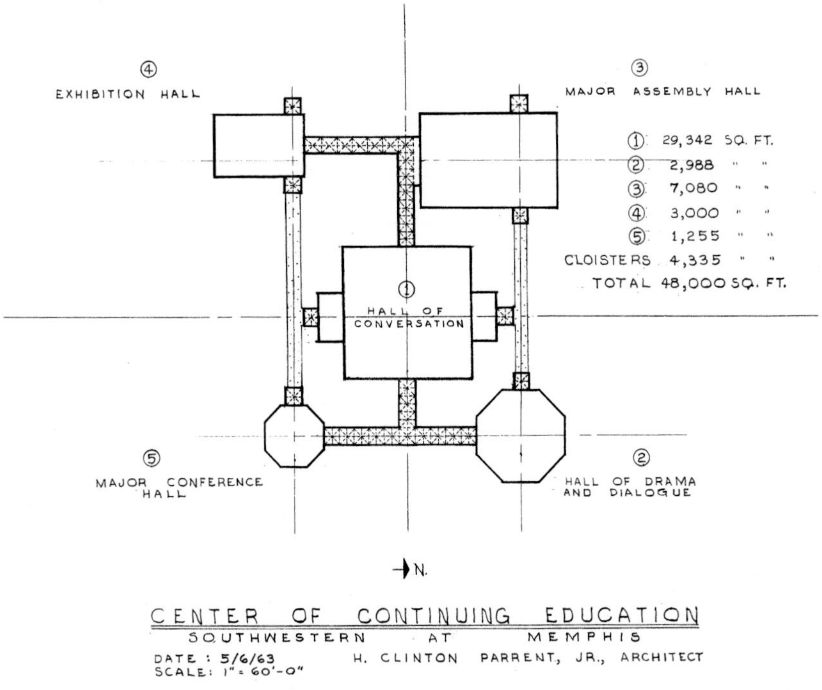

62. Kellogg Center, plan, 6 May 1963.

By 5 May of the same year, this pentagonal plan had been fleshed out into "Scheme B," expanded most notably with the addition of a second story featuring ten "discussion rooms" clustered around a balcony overlooking the Forum, plus six offices and a lounge added atop the entrance wing. The total square footage was estimated at 10,152 for the first floor and 7,624 for the second, all to be constructed at a total cost of $471,064 (or $26 per square foot). But it was soon perceived that the single building would not be large enough or flexible enough to incorporate all the various assemblies and discussion groups.

Exactly two years after Scheme B, Parrent and Rhodes had refined the plan (Fig. 62) to include a five-part building complex consisting of a large central "Hall of Conversation" (29,342 square feet) connected by cloistered walkways to two octagonal halls (the larger being the "Hall of Drama and Dialogue") and the two rectangular buildings, an exhibition hall, and a large assembly hall—all totaling 48,000 square feet. The drawings that survive of "Scheme C" (Fig. 63) from the summer and autumn of 1963 show that Parrent retained the chapter house motif of the earliest plan. By the time the professional rendering (Fig. 64) went off to the Kellogg Foundation in Battle Creek, the Mallory-like central block had been increased by an extra floor (to four stories), and one of the rectangular corner pavilions had been transformed into an octagon.

Given the limited evidence of a few drawings, it is difficult to know exactly how this project might have turned out. Even so, the college architecture to date, and specifically Parrent's work up to and beyond 1963, certainly make it fair to assume that the Kellogg Center for Continuing Education would have been an intriguing addition to a handsome campus. At the very least, the drawings for Kellogg demonstrate Parrent's remarkable ability to combine contemporary needs with respect for the college's desire to maintain the Gothic style.

Within a year of the disappointment over the failure of the Kellogg Center, Parrent had a chance to return to the less demanding task of a new men's dormitory (Fig. 65). Originally called North, the dorm was renamed in 1968 to honor Alfred C. Glassell, a Louisiana oil man and alumnus who had contributed more than a million dollars to Southwestern.

Located to the west of Moore Moore Infirmary, Glassell was the first dorm that was unconnected to the existing residence halls. Also, unlike the usual I plan of the others, Glassell's configuration is something like a modified U with unequal length arms—its unusual shape having been determined in order to preserve some existing trees. Glassell felicitously continues the long expanse of pudding stone and gray-green slate and the carefully orchestrated rhythms of the limestone-trimmed fenestration in the best Klauder-at-Princeton manner; there is not a curved line anywhere—even the doorways are straight. Built in the normal two calendar years' time (1964–1965), Glassell almost broke Southwestern's iconoclastic precedent when during construction "a stonecutter of medieval mind carved a fair likeness of President Rhodes" and affixed it over the main entrance of the new dorm. "The Colossus of Rhodes," as it was dubbed, was quickly removed at the subject's behest.[31]

During the half-dozen years that Dr. Rhodes, the reluctant gargoyle, was trying to obtain funding for the Kellogg Center and college architect Parrent was working on its design, the college was able to realize a less ambitious but probably more needed building. As Professor Roper tells us:

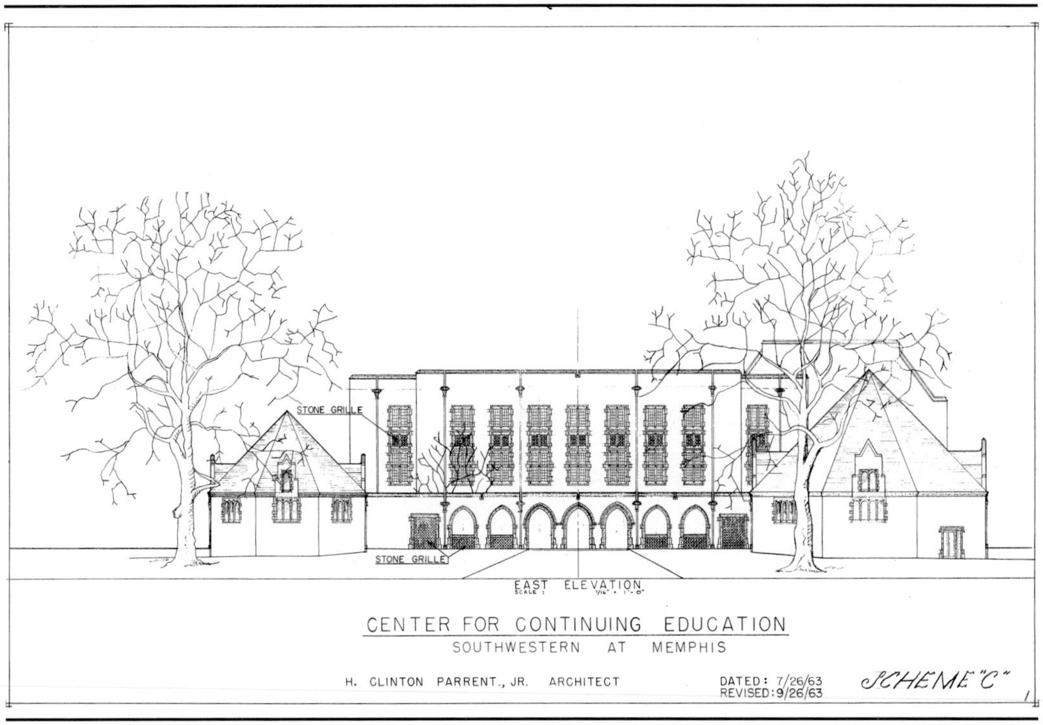

63. Kellogg Center, Scheme C, July-September 1963.

From the student point of view there was little doubt about which prospective building had top priority. The grubbiness of the Lynx Lair under Neely Hall, with its overhead pipes and its underfoot grime and grit, not to mention its general basement gloom and limited space, had aroused an intense desire for a civilized Student Center which might serve as a suitable headquarters for campus life.[32]

Students began raising money in 1958, and plans for the building were unveiled three years later, although it was not until January 1963 that a gift of $270,000 from Thomas W. Briggs made the building a reality. Mr. Briggs, the founder of Welcome Wagon International, actually presented the college with a thirty-four-acre tract of land, the sale of which contributed more than half of the building's eventual cost. Ground was broken in February 1965, and in their typically efficient manner, Parrent and his trusted contractors, Canfield, Badgett and Scarborough, were able to have the building ready for occupancy by May of the following year.

Housing a new Lynx Lair, bookstore, post office, lounges, game rooms, office,

64. Kellogg Center, rendering by Schell Lewis, 1963.

65. Glassell Hall, 1964–1965.

and language laboratory, the Thomas Briggs Student Center (Fig. 66) occupies a site a hundred yards north of Palmer Hall. While we can be amused by Dr. Roper's description of the new student union with its "two somewhat squat towers, suggesting a sandstone Rheims with perhaps a bit of pituitary trouble,"[33] the handsome student center is another version of the Southwestern I-plan building, but with two extra towers inserted for emphasis on the inside front corners. Naturally, the building shares similarities with the collegiate work of Cram and Klauder that Parrent so admired, but the student center is more than an exercise in architectural nostalgia. In Parrent's office files are clippings of dozens of contemporary student unions throughout the country—most of which with their flat roofs, aluminum mullions, and colored enamel walls must look terribly dated less than a generation later, an eventuality for which the architect had obviously planned. The steel frame that Parrent employed (Fig. 68) also reminds us that the designer was not bound to old-fashioned building technology.

The Student Center had been part of the 1944 plan, but Dr. Diehl's original campus scheme of 1923 had included three buildings for the sciences, only the first of which had been built. Thus, it was appropriate that Clinton Parrent's last project at Southwestern—and one that was announced at President Rhodes's farewell dinner in 1965—be the science center envisioned by Charles

66. Briggs Student Center, 1965–1966.

Diehl. The Frazier Jelke Science Center, begun late in 1966 and dedicated two years later, was the most expensive building project by far that the college had ever undertaken. Its $2,800,000 cost came from the Ford Foundation and a campaign that included a $500,000 contribution from the Frazier Jelke Foundation, "which said it was prompted to do so because of the Ford Foundation's view of Southwestern as 'one of the great institutions in the country.'"[34]

The new science complex also offered the architect one of his thorniest challenges, testing his ability to successfully

67. Proposed Student Union Building, 1945.

68. Briggs Student Center, under construction.

place contemporary functions behind traditional façades. The most immediate problem was location. Even though the plan of 1944 showed a central quadrangle (with Palmer Hall as the southern side), it had been decided when Briggs was designed that the new student center would face an open terrace with a view to Palmer. There was also the difficulty of the very size of the science-mathematics facilities (eighty-five thousand square feet) and their technical requirements, not to mention that the architect had at that moment only two draftsmen in his office, and one of those was part-time. So Parrent called in his old friend from student days at Penn, J. Roy Carroll, Jr., as an associate.[35]

Clinton Parrent sketched a plot plan, dated 10 June 1965, which shows a building about twice the size of Kennedy, and extending northward from that building to a point considerably beyond the Student Center. No renderings of this Kennedy extension idea have survived, but soon thereafter Roy Carroll came up with the ingenious solution of placing laboratories and classrooms beneath an open plaza that connected two towerlike buildings.[36] This design provided the needed space, modern facilities, and two Gothic buildings that, along with Briggs and Kennedy,[37] help enclose the large space behind Palmer (Figs. 69–70).

Both the Mathematics Building (which houses the Buckman Library as well as the

Department of Mathematics) and Rhodes Tower (housing the former president's Physics Department, and affectionately dubbed "Peyton Place" by the students) are large rectangular cubes whose very blockiness and lack of softening curves recall the similar towers of Bellingrath and Voorhies. They also appear to be fortified, like some of Edward I's castles that have strayed far west of the Welsh borders. The thought of lasers and quarks in a Gothic building may at first raise a mild eyebrow, but it is no more incongruous than having hundreds of years of Cambridge architecture as home to one of the world's most renowned science faculties. The modern metaphors seem strong at first, especially at Rhodes Tower, which, thanks to the advice of Professor Jack Taylor, was planned like an aircraft carrier with its service island to one side. Yet, the abiding backdrop of the Arkansas sandstone is still here. And, just as the Gothic of Oxford and Cambridge was not created all at one time or even in one specific style, Parrent's "ivory towers" range from the fortifications of Rhodes and Bellingrath to the domesticity of Moore and the monasticism of Voorhies.

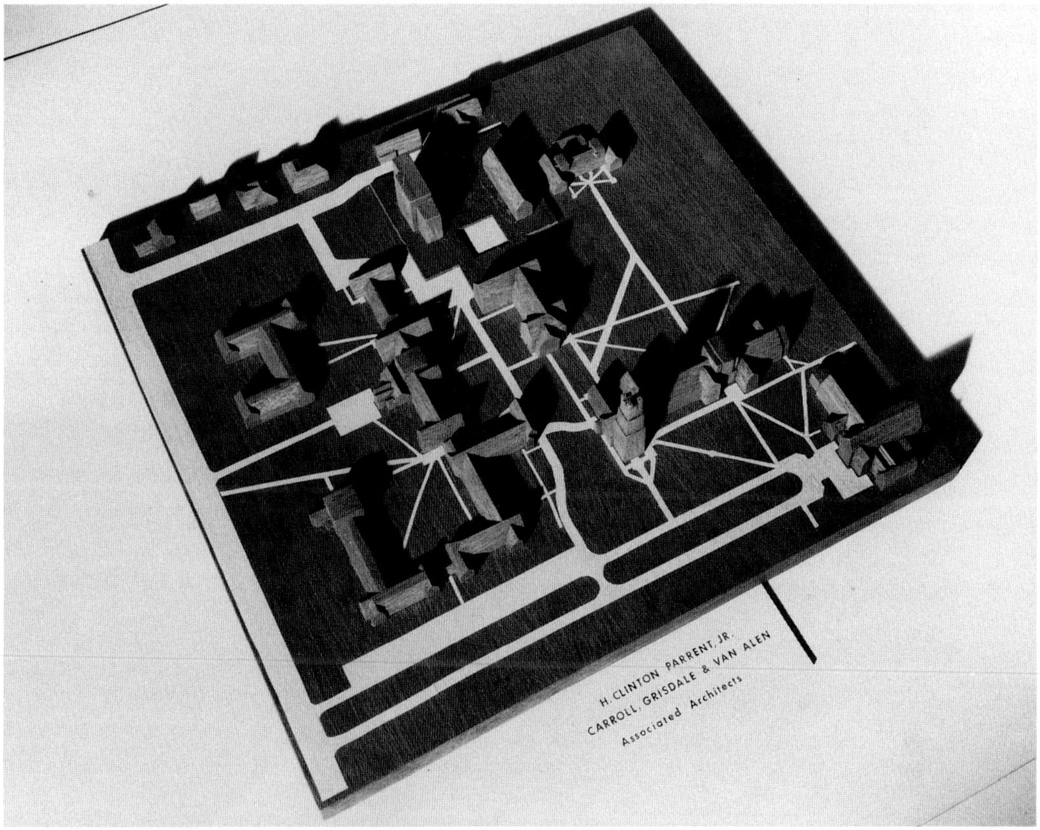

69. Frazier Jelke Science Center, model, 1965.

If the happy marriage of Rhodes and Mathematics with Briggs and Kennedy causes delight and demonstrates their architect's flexibility and inventiveness, the below-ground Biology Department's home is less successful. This is actually a non-building, and the flat concrete plaza that serves as roof for the laboratories and classrooms approaches a starkness that is an all-too-familiar aspect of many Modernist buildings of the late 1960s. The light wells, the amphitheater on the Palmer side, and the concept of going below ground to maintain the integrity of the campus were all inspired ideas, but the unnecessarily bleak plaza awaits the further touch of a sensitive landscape architect or sculptor. Given Clinton Parrent's artistry at Southwestern, one might wish to conclude that the plaza's design took shape following his death from a heart attack on 30 September 1967.

There was one other building to be erected in the 1960s, but the passing of H. Clin-

70. Frazier Jelke Science Center.

ton Parrent marked the end of an era that began with Southwestern's move to Memphis. With the exception of Burrow Library, the entire campus had been shaped by Henry Hibbs and his apprentice-assistant-associate successor. They began their work for Southwestern at a time when the Collegiate Gothic style was at its height, but at the time of their passing Dr. Diehl's chosen mode of expression was very much out of favor. Yet, they kept their faith, and they demonstrably showed that Gothic could be as functional and alive as any other style. From Palmer Hall to Frazier Jelke Science Center, these two architects created this most beautiful of college campuses, and that is no mean achievement.

5 Dr. Daughdrill's Chariot of Fire

An organization ought to know its values and where it wants to go. Once you start setting goals—and a goal is a hope with a deadline—something almost mystical takes place in any community of people. They begin to work toward its happening and essentially invent their own future.

—James H. Daughdrill, Jr.

71. James H. Daughdrill, Jr.

James H. Daughdrill, Jr., Southwestern's third larger-than-life steward, assumed the presidency of the college in 1973. Dr. Daughdrill graduated from Emory University, but like Woodrow Wilson, he attended Davidson, and like Charles Diehl, he is a man of the cloth. Before becoming a Presbyterian clergyman, this tall Georgian had been a successful carpet manufacturer. And, like the Memphis college's founder, James Daughdrill came to Southwestern with an understanding of the crucial role that good architecture plays in the spiritual and physical life of the college. While the new president would institute a variety of changes—including the renaming of the school as Rhodes—he was committed to fostering the college's growth while maintaining its Gothic legacy.

When Peyton Rhodes relinquished the reins of Southwestern, the rather stark Physics Tower that would carry his name and the somewhat disquieting Frazier Jelke Science Center were under construction. And while it is the nature of history to be less sure of the recent past, one can say that the years between Dr. Rhodes's retirement and the accession of Dr. Daughdrill were ones of architectural uncertainty.

Dr. Rhodes's immediate successor was John David Alexander, a Rhodes Scholar and a Presbyterian clergyman who stayed to see the 1960s through before becoming president of Pomona College in California. William Bowden, who was a Southwestern alumnus like his predecessor (although his graduate work was undertaken at another Modern Gothic campus, the University of Chicago), served less than a third of a decade. Thus, while neither president can be called one of the college's builder-leaders, the construction of their brief tenure is part of the Southwestern-Rhodes story.

Williford Hall (Fig. 72), a large women's dormitory just to the north of the Voorhies-Townsend-Trezevant complex, was one of two buildings designed during the Alexander presidency and was the last building of the 1960s.[1] Excepting Burrow Library, Williford was the first building on campus that was not the work of either Henry Hibbs or Clinton Parrent. The designers were McGehee-Nicholson Associates, a Memphis firm whose principals were friends of Dr. Rhodes. To the untrained eye, Williford would seem to be from the same mold as the other women's dorms, but there are subtleties that mark this as being by different hands. Most noticeable is the fact that the new dormitory is more varied in its massing; its silhouette is far more complicated that those of its predecessors. Also, Williford lacks the usual broad band of sheltering slate, for it has three stories (with less roof) instead of two plus an attic story in the Princeton-at-Southwestern manner. McGehee-Nicholson's expertise was not in Collegiate Gothic—few designers had Hibbs and Parrent's training by the Nixon years—but they deftly managed not to disturb the attractiveness of the "women's side" of campus.

72. Williford Hall, 1968–1969.

The Southwestern trademark of long expanses of slate roof virtually unbroken save for simple dormers was recovered in S. Dewitt Clough Hall, which was dedicated in the autumn of 1970 (Fig. 73). Housing the departments of Art, Anthropology, and Psychology, as well as the Edward J. Meeman Center for Continuing Education, this large and expensive building (it cost exactly half what the Science Center had) was made possible through the generosity of a Chicagoan whose sister had taught high school art in Memphis. As his widow recalled, "At the end of every year, my husband would make out a list of what he wanted to contribute to and how much money he had available for gifts. One day he said, 'We ought to do something for that college in Memphis that has Jessie's things.' And he did."[2] "Jessie's things" are a collection of works of art, particularly Japanese prints, gathered partly during a 1919 trip around the world undertaken by Miss Clough and two of her students, Floy and Etta Hanson. After Miss Clough's death in 1940, the Hanson sisters presented their mentor's objets d'art to Southwestern, and Dewitt Clough gave the building primarily to house his sister's legacy.

Clough was designed by Wells Awsumb of the old and respected Memphis firm of George Awsumb & Sons and a Southwestern alumnus. Awsumb placed the new humanities building at right angles to Palmer and to the north of Burrow Library, siting it where the Liberal Arts Building would have formed the east side of the central quadrangle in the 1944 plan. Unlike McGehee-Nicholson, Awsumb understood the Klauder-Hibbs-Parrent aesthetic and employed their traditional scheme of a long building intersected by smaller elements.

73. Clough Hall, 1968–1970.

He also understood the importance of the mass of the slate roof, the subtle rhythm of the right angle, and the curveless fenestration of the older buildings. But because the architect also abandoned what Roper calls "the hallowed mullions" in favor of "large contemporary panes," a sort of college mythology has grown up that Clough is, in Peyton Rhodes's words, "not in keeping with the other buildings."[3] In fact, Clough is more in keeping with its neighbors than Williford, and no less so than Mallory, a medieval basketball court. The larger windows with their contrasting dark recesses create a stronger sense of modeling, with results—as the architect no doubt intended—that are at once medieval and contemporary. Clough Hall reminds us again how flexible and modern the Gothic style can be.

That the transformation of the Gothic of Oxford and Cambridge to the latter half of the twentieth century was deftly accomplished by Wells Awsumb is forcefully brought home by one look at the other new building of the 1970s.[4] The small, administrative Frances Falls Austin Building was constructed in 1979 in a half-timber style, perhaps in hopes that it would seem a continuation of the domestic Gothic of the fraternities nestled just to the west, as well as echo Tuthill Hall immediately to the east. Although planned as a temporary structure, Austin's watered-down Gothic appearance merely demonstrates what other architects employed by Southwestern knew instinctively: that the style used is less important than the underlying architectural principles.

Thus, the arrival of James Daughdrill on the Southwestern campus in 1973 was an important watershed in the architectural destiny of the college. For while English half-timbering (like that attempted at Austin) was not inappropriate to a Collegiate Gothic campus, particularly for small structures like fraternities, Daughdrill was determined that the college pick up again the Diehl-established tradition of demanding the best for the college's physical environment.

With the renovation of the former Zeta Tau Alpha sorority in 1981 into the McCoy Theatre (Fig. 74), a young architect named Metcalf Crump showed that Daughdrill had found an architect sensitive, sophisticated, and learned enough to create the kind of buildings that would respect and enhance Dr. Diehl's dream while meeting the college's current and future needs. Given by Harry B. McCoy, Jr., a millionaire real-estate developer who was

74. McCoy Theatre, 1981.

75. Metcalf Crump and President Daughdrill.

killed at age thirty-seven in 1966 and who left the bulk of his estate for the furthering of the dramatic arts in Memphis, the former sorority lodge was more than doubled in size with the addition of a sixty- by sixty-foot "black box" theatre. This modern stage is cloaked on the exterior with the college's hallmark Arkansas sandstone, but perhaps even more reassuring to partisans of Southwestern's Gothic spirit is the wood-beamed lobby with its welcoming fireplace. It was this imaginative melding of the contemporary with the traditional that convinced President Daughdrill that Met Crump was the man to design the new music building.

At a time when the Gothic Revival has been moribund, if not dead, for decades and when there are virtually no architects working in anything even approaching Gothic, one could well marvel how the college would find a successor to Henry Hibbs and Clinton Parrent. Metcalf Crump is a Memphian and a graduate of Tennessee's other notable Collegiate Gothic school, the University of the South at Sewanee, where he majored in French. But it was a class trip to Europe with the Memphis University School at the age of sixteen that opened his eyes to architecture, especially the glories of Gothic France. France—and the structural engineering of the Gothic cathedral—retained such a fascination for Crump that he took a year off from his studies at the Harvard Graduate School of Design to attend the École des Beaux-Arts in Paris. He received his Master's in architecture from Harvard in 1970 and returned to Memphis, where he and a friend founded the firm of Taylor & Crump Architects.

In less than twenty years, Crump and his office (The Crump Firm since 1985) have become one of the Mid-South's most successful commercial architectural firms. The projects for which Crump has served as principal designer include a score of residential developments, at least two dozen

76. Metcalf Crump, Econocom—USA Corporate Headquarters, Memphis, 1988.

hotels (mostly for the Memphis-based Holiday Inn chain), many commercial buildings and office parks (Fig. 76), and several churches, as well as a variety of educational and environmental master plans. Crump's work so far demonstrates a solid achievement: attractive, contemporary buildings that please their clients and contribute to their surroundings. While renovations like the McCoy Theatre and other rehabilitation projects at Rhodes show an understanding of past architecture, he has resisted the temptation to engage in pastichery.

As good as Met Crump's oeuvre is to date, it might not seem at first all that remarkable. Yet having been trained at Harvard, that hotbed of Modernism and antihistoricism (especially in the late 1960s), and at the ultra-classical French academy (where for years Gothic was hardly mentioned, much less taught), he has managed to fashion a Collegiate Gothic that is appropriate to Southwestern's past and Rhodes's future. Just when skeptics might have declared that Dr. Diehl's Gothic dream was finally over, Dr. Daughdrill encouraged Met Crump to develop a compatible, traditional style that would not be a slavish imitation of the past.

Stone masons spent five months fashioning four hundred and fifty tons of Arkansas sandstone to form the two stories of Hassell Hall, the new music building that was completed in 1983 (Fig. 77). The studios, classrooms, lecture hall, library, and practice rooms that the music department so desperately needed were now housed in what is to be the first component of a quadrangle north of the Student Center. From the outset, Crump saw the music building as a defense "to keep the campus from unraveling."[5]

A long block that pays homage to the Hibbs-Parrent tradition, Hassell nevertheless immediately declares the independence of its designer, while at the same time heralding the Daughdrill era. Hassell's entrance pavilion breaks high into the otherwise unbroken expanse of Vermont slate, rising to a full three stories. The entry arch is echoed by a two-story arched surround, which gives this tower a dense, layered look—this is most definitely not the planar and linear Collegiate Gothic of Charles Klauder and his followers. Furthermore, this prominent entrance is not in the center, but has four bays to its west and three to the right; all but one of the bays are defined by a

77. Hassell Hall, 1983.

sharply gabled parapet that rises above the eave line, while that furthest from the door has a parapet twice as large as its confrères. The result of all this is a variation on the subtle facade-plane relationships already noted in the buildings by Hibbs and Parrent. But while Crump understands and appreciates his predecessors, his work is not an echo of theirs, but rather another instance of the versatility of Collegiate Gothic when shaped by the right hands.

At the same time Daughdrill asked Crump to design the new music building, the president raised the issue of a unified campus master plan. While the plans of the 1920s and 1940s had been more or less followed, it was clear by the early 1980s that an overhaul was needed. The wonderful series of quadrangles that had set the tone at Southwestern had been challenged by the placement of Briggs and the Science Center, and now the unformed north end of campus posed a potentially greater danger of quadrangular disintegration. In order to meet

78. East Hall, 1985.

79. East Hall, elevation drawing.

80. New Dorm, 1986.

that threat (and perhaps having the Science Center in mind), President Daughdrill urged the Board of Trustees to pass a motion in 1983 "that Southwestern maintain its Collegiate Gothic Architecture for all future buildings."[6]

The exploration of the possibilities of Collegiate Gothic at Rhodes in recent years is evident in Met Crump's two new dormitories. Sited east of the Student Center and just north of the Voorhies-Williford compound, East Hall and New Dorm, completed in 1985 and 1986 and connected by a cloister, show that campus Gothic is very much a living style (Figs. 78–80). Some observers might mistakenly think of these buildings as yet another Postmodern phase, a dipping into the past to borrow various pieces of historical styles to decorate other-

81. Refectory West Hall, 1987.

wise modern structures. Rather, East and New (both are awaiting donors, and subsequently permanent names) represent the natural evolution of the Collegiate Gothic from Klauder through Hibbs, Parrent, and Awsumb to the present and beyond. And, like his predecessors, Crump uses a Gothic vocabulary to evoke medieval memories, but he does so only after he has studied and mastered the complete language.[7]

In keeping with Daughdrill's intention to protect and continue the Gothic of the Southwestern past, East and New are among Rhodes College's most traditional structures, for they seem the most historical, the most reminiscent of the Oxbridge models. Nevertheless, they are also free and inventive. While respecting the massing and fenestration—and the almighty slate roofs—of the Hibbs-Parrent buildings, Crump has incorporated some revolutionary changes for Rhodes, particularly in his use of curved lines. The one-and-a-half-story boiler house and laundry pavilion at the south end of

82. Refectory West Hall, interior.

83. TAC Master Plan, April 1986.

East not only breaks the college's rarely challenged 58-degree rule of slope, but it does so with an almost capricious bell-cast curve that reaches nearly to the ground, all delightfully recalling a thatched roof or the early seventeenth-century Arlington Row at Bibury in Gloucestershire. In fact, this prospect of East and New recalls the unpretentious vernacular Gothic of the Cotswolds as much as it does the English universities. The architect, however, does provide towers to echo those of Voorhies and Palmer—and that on New Hall even sports an entire curved facade. The joyous sense of whimsy, or at least lightheartedness, is reinforced when one notices that the "Colossus of Rhodes" installed surreptitiously at Glassell has now found a legitimate home high up the parapet at New Hall.[8]

Just as Clinton Parrent was called upon to expand Henry Hibbs's original dining hall, thirty years later Metcalf Crump made a major expansion to the college's dining facilities. Unlike the "clean slate" he had at New and East, here the architect had the difficult problem of inserting the large single-room refectory into the constricted area behind Burrow-Neely and north of the original men's dormitories. The exterior (Fig. 81) repeats the rhythm of the windows on Burrow, but the single gable entrance has the characteristic Crump form. Most important, this dignified facade closes the space behind Bellingrath-Ellett-White and

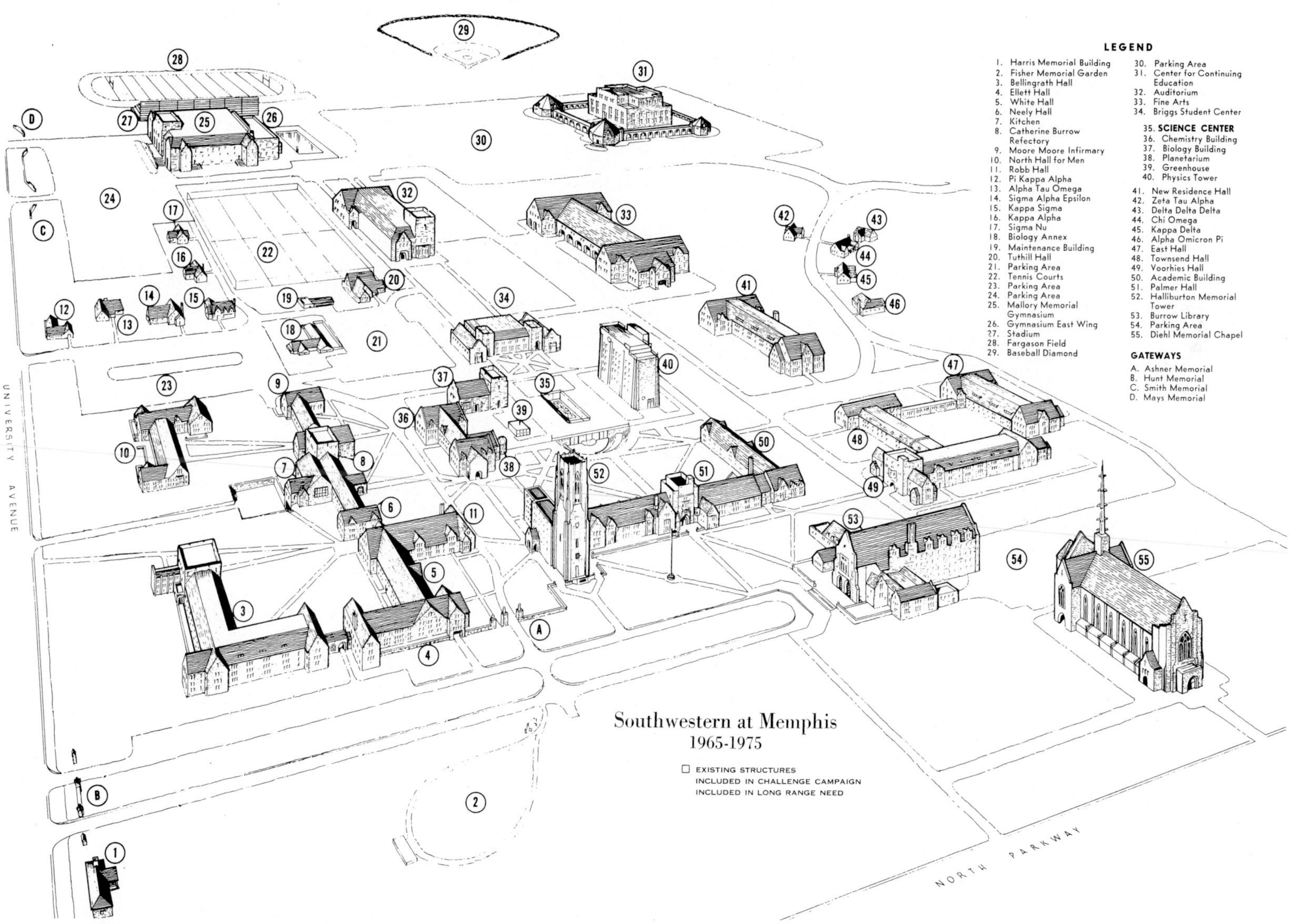

84. Harland-Bartholomew Master Plan, 1964.

thus finally completes one of Dr. Diehl's dreamed-for quadrangles.[9]

The successful low massing of the outside unfortunately constrains the interior (Fig. 82), where the necessary large space is somewhat awkwardly proportioned. The broad ceiling beams are no longer than, say, those of the great halls at Oxbridge or Princeton, but the architect did not have the requisite height to produce entirely convincing proportions. Even so, the paneling, which duplicates that in the old refectory, along with the 1924 chandeliers, college portraits, and banners, help make for a pleasant gathering place.

The concern for a new master plan voiced by President Daughdrill and Met Crump in 1981 was translated into action in 1985 when it was decided to invite ten design and planning firms to make proposals; two firms were chosen for interviews: Skidmore, Owings & Merrill (SOM) and The Architects Collaborative (TAC).[10] It might come as a surprise that Rhodes would consider firms with such Modernist credentials, but the physical planning process is different from the design of buildings, and planners had to be sought whose appreciation of the Collegiate Gothic style was of less importance than their understanding of the underlying principles of campus planning. The Architects Collaborative was founded by Walter Gropius of Bauhaus fame—hardly the firm one would think sympathetic to Rhodes's architectural philosophy (or as Robert Stern remarked, "Hiring TAC for Rhodes is like asking Mae West to play Ophelia"). On the other hand, Daughdrill was determined to avoid the inhuman scale of SOM's much-criticized United States Air Force Academy in Colorado Springs, and he certainly did not want a recreation of their concrete wilderness at the University of Illinois at Chicago. Yet TAC, with the strong endorsement of Met Crump, showed a respect for what Rhodes had accomplished and expressed a willingness to work with the college. Philosophical considerations aside, Rhodes deserves credit for considering some of the better-known planners—not unlike Southwestern's desire to obtain Charles Klauder as campus architect in 1922.

The College Master Plan submitted by TAC in April 1986 is, after all, only a planning document. As the planners themselves noted, "The plan is evolutionary rather than revolutionary." While the plan should speak for itself, certain characteristics can be reviewed briefly.

Primarily, the TAC plan (Fig. 83) builds upon "what has already been accomplished in the way of attractive academic quadrangles," and it sensibly excludes automobiles from the center of the campus, something the 1964 plan by the Memphis firm of Harland-Bartholomew did not (Fig. 84). The chief feature of the TAC scheme is the creation of three new quadrangles:

(1) Two new dormitories south of Voorhies, facing an expanded Burrow Library, and joined by a Social Science Hall south of Burrow and parallel to Palmer (Met Crump has designed this last structure, to be called Buckman Hall; see Fig. 85).

(2) A Humanities Building west of Buckman will be attached at right angles to an Administration Building. When completed this will close a newly formed quadrangle whose center will be the Diehl Memorial.

(3) Hassell Hall will have an addition, also at right angles, and will face an L-shaped academic building, which along with a large auditorium to the west side of the music building will form a quadrangle with Briggs (which may itself be expanded).

The plan also shows Glassell II, a building that will form a U-shaped court with the existing Glassell Hall and Moore Moore Infirmary. Eventually, these will be joined by a Physical Plant Maintenance Building beyond an expanded McCoy Theatre, a gymnasium addition, and a Faculty Club and Inn attached to the Harris Gate Lodge. Across University Street, the first phase of another housing complex, University Quadrangle, has already begun. Called Spann Place, this is the work of Memphis designers MMH Hall, Architects (Fig. 86).[11]

As we have seen with the earlier master plans, such schemes are almost always changed. The 1964 plan, for example, showed a large chapel between Burrow and North Parkway, while Walk Jones's

85. Buckman Hall, rendering of south front.

86. Spann Place, 1987.

design for five faculty houses in the 1920s was never realized. But some aspects of the TAC plan are worth noting. Although none of the quadrangles is closed at the corners as in the plans of the 1920s and 1940s, the quadrangle remains the key element in Rhodes's campus design. Few if any of the new structures will be more than three stories tall, sandstone and slate remain the materials of choice, and there is continued emphasis on arboriculture. In sum, the TAC Master Plan seems to further Charles Diehl's very aims dating from the move to Memphis—and which were reaffirmed by Peyton Rhodes and James Daughdrill: a humane and domestically scaled environment reminiscent of the quadrangles, lawns, and quiet corners of Oxford and Cambridge.

6 And Was Jerusalem Builded Here

Rhodes maintains a campus that is second to none in its design, function and beauty. Students benefit because elegant architecture inspires us, broadens the mind, expands the consciousness to beauty and harmony, and reminds us of the history and breadth of learning . . . . Such a campus shapes the quality of education and provides students a constant vision of excellence.

—Mission Statement adopted by Board of Trustees, 1986

87. Diehl Court, 1983.

There is no conclusion to the architectural history of Rhodes College. Readers who yearn for tidy assessments or closing reflections should perhaps look to the sesquicentennial of the college in 1998, a year that will also mark a quarter century of James Daughdrill's presidency.

Nevertheless, this study has perhaps challenged the common belief that Rhodes architecture is composed of buildings that are all alike. If Rhodes were as unified and as consistent as is sometimes held, the campus would be a very static place indeed. Rhodes was built not as some sort of pastiche, but as a reinterpretation of a style associated with our history and with learning. Architects or developers or a people who literally try to imitate the past often end up with a Disneyworld or a Williamsburg—places that may be delightful to visit but that have little to do with history. As attractive as Rhodes may be, it is not a stage set; its purpose is the pursuit of truth rather than play-acting. Even the trustees' avowed commitment to the Collegiate Gothic style is less to an aesthetic than to an ethic: that the architecture should express the ideals of the college.

"Therefore when we build, let us think that we build forever." That statement by John Ruskin, probably the most influential art critic of modern times, is invoked at Rhodes in support of the college building program. But an equally apt epigram of that romantic lover of Gothic reminds us that we can live and even worship without architecture, but "we cannot remember without architecture." The architecture of Rhodes is about memory. It is about image and symbolism, about how a place looks, and about a sense of place.

One game that has been especially popular in recent years has been that of rating colleges. Favorable as they often are to Rhodes, such ratings are not the same as serious inquiries into what makes one college or university better than another. The important intangibles that give a certain college "spirit" are not quantifiable, like test scores. Yet, often the perception of quality is shaped by the physical setting; like it or not, we unconsciously rate an educational institution by what it looks like. Visualize some of the most respected American colleges and universities—say, Harvard, Yale, Princeton, Duke, Michigan, Stanford, Chicago, Dartmouth, Bryn Mawr, Oberlin—and it is almost impossible to recollect one that is not physically attractive, a campus where good architecture is part of the educational mission, even if not consciously avowed as at Rhodes.

Architecture is the result of decisions made by many people. It may be careful or haphazard, the result may not be what the patron expected or the designer hoped for, but it is rarely accidental. As the most public art—and that carrying the most responsibility—a great work of architecture is harder to achieve than a great painting or a novel. A brilliant scheme from the mind of an imaginative designer can be crippled by shoddy materials, by a less-than-understanding client, or by a lack of funds to realize the idea or maintain it if it is built.

88. Diehl statue and Rollow Avenue of Oaks.

Rhodes College is one of the places where good architects, superb materials, unflagging maintenance, an enlightened client, and an appreciative community were all present. As with a great beauty who has intelligence and personality, it is not necessary to distinguish between the physical presence of Rhodes and its personality-spirit-soul, because they have become, as Dr. Diehl dreamed, the same thing.

In October 1983 the college dedicated a memorial to Charles Diehl (Fig. 87). It was designed by sculptor Ted Rust and architects James Williamson and Carl Awsumb, and the nine-foot bronze statue depicts the former president standing, wearing his academic robes and pince-nez. Backed by Burrow Library and framed by the entrance tower of Palmer Hall, the statue has become one of the familiar images of Rhodes, no longer the struggling little college that Dr. Diehl moved to Memphis.

Charles Diehl's dream has become his legacy. His vision melded the academic and architectural heritage of Oxford and Princeton with the religious spirit of John Witherspoon and Woodrow Wilson, and he joined the best traditions of the log college and the high table into a dream whose physical expression is the architecture of Rhodes College.

Appendix: Fraternity Row

The College will assign a piece of ground on the campus for each fraternity or sorority, upon which that fraternity or sorority may build a club house of the lodge type, but not a residential house . . . . The plans and elevations of these houses must be approved by the architect and the President of the College. The houses are to be of the same material as the other buildings, and are to be harmonious with the whole. They are to be erected of rubble stone, which will be supplied at reasonable cost by the College, this stone to be laid in the wall the same way as it is laid in other buildings; the same type of metal windows are to be used; there is to be the same type of roof, that is the same quality and color of slate. The lodges are to be built in narrow units, of not more than twenty feet span of roof, and the roof is to have a pitch of fifty-two degrees.

—President Diehl

89. Alpha Tau Omega, before enlargement.

Charles Diehl, with his usual thoroughness and concern for the overall appearance of his Gothic dream, prescribed certain rules regarding the design of the fraternities and sororities. In so doing he deferred to the Greek societies' financial independence and their need for individual identities, although one might have thought that Diehl would have insisted on their being grouped in a social quadrangle. Nevertheless, the six fraternities and five sororities built between the late 1920s and the early 1950s contribute to the bucolic collegiate atmosphere of Rhodes. Yet, despite their importance to the life of the college, the social clubs are not well documented, and most of their designers are not remembered.

Kappa Sigma, built in 1928–1930, was the first permanent lodge built at Southwestern. "Old English in style,"[1] the stone-trimmed Tudor doorway and pair of projecting gables provided a more appropriate Gothic demeanor than the log house that Chi Omega sorority purchased in 1926 and moved to the campus. Kappa Sigma was the first of a row of fraternities that runs to University Street; they are Tudor domestic in style and of uniform height (all of the college's social houses are one story or a story and a half), although each is slightly varied in its use of gables, wings, and chimneys.

Just to the west of Kappa Sigma is Sigma Alpha Epsilon ("under construction" in 1933),[2] and then Alpha Tau Omega, built in 1938. The latter's front gable is a later addition to a rather plain rectangular house unadorned except for a brick Jacobean chimney stack (Fig. 89). Completing the row and framing an entrance from University Street is Pi Kappa Alpha (Fig. 90), dedicated in 1938 by Henry St. George Tucker, presiding bishop of the Episcopal Church.

Kappa Sigma also formed the southern end of a shorter row including Kappa Alpha and Sigma Nu. An unidentified architect's sketch of Kappa Alpha appeared in the May-June 1934 issue of the *Southwestern Alumni Magazine,* and the accompanying article noted that the lodge "will cost $8,500. It will be Gothic in design . . . . The ceiling beams will be exposed, giving the Tudor appearance." As built, Kappa Alpha retained the single front gable and prominent central chimney, but the half-tim-

90. Pi Kappa Alpha.

91. Sigma Nu.

bered porch shown in the drawing was omitted. Sigma Nu, built in 1936, is the most overtly Gothic in detail, featuring a Tudor drip molding above the entrance and a triple-arched arcade on the south facade (Fig. 91); Herbert M. Burnham was the architect.

Keeping with the division of the campus between male and female quarters, the sororities were clustered on the east side, just north of the women's dormitories.

The rustic cabin that Chi Omega acquired has already been mentioned, but the first sorority constructed on the campus was Alpha Omicron Pi, "built in English design in 1927."[3] Despite Diehl's strictures for the design of the lodges, the exterior walls were stucco, with the otherwise ubiquitous Arkansas sandstone used only for the entranceway and flanking chimney. At any rate, the chapter outgrew this modest beginning, and in 1950 Jeter Eason of the firm of Eason, Anthony, McKinney and Cox designed "a five-room Gothic style building," which did have the requisite stone walls.[4]

Zeta Tau Alpha's original chapter house, opened in 1931, also broke the Gothic-in-stone prescription and was constructed of white clapboard. Ironically, the wooden lodge was struck by lightning and burned to the ground in 1946. The attractive masonry replacement, built at a cost of twenty-five thousand dollars and completed in the spring of 1950, became the McCoy Theatre three decades later (Fig. 74).

92. Kappa Delta, 1928.

The other three sororities—Chi Omega's replacement for its Davy Crockett–like homeplace, Delta Delta Delta (completed in 1933), and Kappa Delta (completed in 1928)—are more in keeping with Diehl's hopes for the Hellenic houses. Kappa Delta is especially attractive, with its rubble walls and timbered lych gate entrance (Fig. 92).

Unfortunately, several of the lodges no longer thwart the weather with rich Vermont slate; without it the lodges look more like suburban "Stockbroker's Tudor" houses of the period than the Cotswold cottages they were intended to recall. On balance, however, the fraternities and sororities help maintain the domestic scale that was so much a part of Diehl's academical village.

There is one intriguing architectural project associated with fraternities, a somewhat mysterious tale that can be followed through the pages of *Southwestern News* from 1946 to 1954: the evolution of PiKA's national headquarters.

In the January 1946 issue of *Southwestern News,* it was announced that the "campus is being considered as a possible site for the proposed $250,000 War Memorial of Pi Kappa Alpha." Accompanying this news was a rendering in the 1940s Hibbs-Parrent style for a building not unlike that proposed for Briggs the year before (Fig. 93). In addition to the national offices, this monumental Gothic structure would contain "an auditorium, a museum to house the historical relics of Pi Kappa Alpha, and a lounge in which fraternities and sororities may meet for social events."

In September of that year, *Southwestern News* reported that the national convention of PiKA had voted to accept the gift of two acres of land from the college at the corner of University and North Parkway on which to build their new headquarters (the University of Virginia and Northwestern were the principal rivals for the site). By March 1947 it was reported that "architect's plans . . . will soon be released," but as is so often the case, the architect was not named. However, the February 1948 *Southwestern News* provided an architect's sketch of a more modest, and far more Tudor-looking, national headquarters building. Paul E. Crider of Columbus, Ohio, gets credit for the design, and, given the more typical fraternity appearance of the drawing, one wonders if he specialized in PiKA houses.[5]

This national headquarters saga had a surprising and somewhat unfortunate end-

93. Pi Kappa Alpha War Memorial, rendering by Clinton Parrent (?), 1946.

94. Pi Kappa Alpha, national headquarters by George Mahoney, under construction, 1945.

ing with regard to Southwestern's stylistic campus unity. In April 1954, *Southwestern News* carried a construction photograph of an unprepossessing brick structure that could pass for a large "Colonial" home in an expensive new development or a suburban bank (Fig. 94).

The building is patterned after the Governor's Palace in Williamsburg, Virginia—doubtless because the architect, Mr. George Mahoney, of Memphis, a graduate of the University of Virginia where the Alpha chapter is located, admires Williamsburg architecture and feels that it is appropriate for the home of PiKA to suggest the state of the fraternity's birth.

The possible intrafraternity politics, economics, or simply poor architectural judgment that led from the suitable Hibbs-Parrent formula to the more picturesque but equally welcome home by Crider to the banality of Mahoney's cardboard cutout of "Developer's Georgian" is not the purview of this study.[6] The difference in style is less important than the fact that the Georgian PiKA is just not good architecture; it is characterized by a certain gawkiness, and its proportional relationships lack authority. Nevertheless, Mahoney's work (now returned to the college as the Meeman Center for Special Studies) can serve as a reminder of what might have happened had Southwestern not adhered to its consistent architectural program.

Notes

Chapter 2: The Gothic Quest of Dr. Diehl

1. W. Raymond Cooper, *Southwestern at Memphis, 1848–1948* (Richmond, 1949), pp. 13–14. Clarksville Academy became Montgomery Masonic College in 1848 and Southwestern Presbyterian University in 1875.

2. Ibid., p. 10; the quotation is from the editor of the *Jeffersonian,* the school newspaper. According to Cooper, the designer of the Castle was "the well-known architect G. B. Vannoy of Gallatin"; nevertheless, a contemporary account (Wilkins Tannehill, "Masonic College of Tennessee," *Portfolio,* 1848–1849, pp. 270–71) cites J. H. Ingraham as the architect of the building and notes that working drawings were made by Vannoy.

3. Quoted in Charles E. Diehl, "Moving a College" (text of a paper read at a meeting of the Egyptians, 15 October 1956), p. 2.

4. *Princeton Alumni Weekly,* 13 December 1902, pp. 199–200.

5. Diehl, "The Ideals of Southwestern," *Southwestern Bulletin* 13 (December 1925): 7, 10. Charles I. Diehl, the founder's son, recalls, "Father was no Anglophile, but he preferred the English university system to the German system . . . . Father's preference for Gothic buildings was probably due to some extent to his years at Princeton, though I don't recall his ever saying so, nor did he ever say that Woodrow Wilson influenced his architectural preference. I think Father chose Gothic because of its beauty, its variety, its adaptability, and its permanence" (letter to author, 10 November 1987). It would be surprising if Diehl were not familiar with the writings of Cram, particularly such books as *The Gothic Quest* (1907), *The Ministry of Art* (1914), and *The Substance of the Gothic* (1919), not to mention his many articles and reviews, as well as his editorship of *Commonweal* and *Christian Art.* In *The Gothic Quest,* Cram noted, "I believe that art—that is, concrete and absolute beauty, acting as a system of spiritual and psychological influence—is perhaps the greatest teaching agency, the greatest because the most subtle and penetrating in its power, man has ever developed" (p. 217). While Diehl certainly did not subscribe to Cram's snobbish Anglo-Catholicism, he clearly shared the architect's belief that education in the liberal arts, though perhaps changed in details, was based on age-old principles that were as valid in twentieth-century Memphis as in medieval Oxford or classical Athens. In his autobiography, *My Life in Architecture* (1936), Cram wrote that he had built the Princeton Graduate College in a style that was both traditional and modern in connotation "consistent with the preservation of historic and cultural continuity that I am pursuaded is fundamental to all educational and ecclesiastical work" (p. 122). Cram, a contemporary of Frank Lloyd Wright, was a leader of the traditionalist architectural camp. (Cram was an able designer in other styles, especially the Georgian.) A complex and contradictory figure, Cram was both founder of the Medieval Academy of America and first chairman of the Boston City Planning Commission. See Douglass Shand Tucci, *Ralph Adams Cram: American Medievalist,* published by the Boston Public Library in 1975 as a companion to an exhibition on Cram; also, the same author's *Church Building in Boston 1920–1970* (Concord, N.H., 1974).

6. Diehl, "Moving a College," p. 9. Charles Diehl "was a combination of White Knight and the U.S. Cavalry . . . . Razzle-dazzle was not the Diehl way: he believed in first things first—start with high standards of education and leave the rest to a Providence which he knew to be firmly on the side of higher learning" (James E. Roper, "Southwestern at Memphis, 1848–1891," *Tennessee Historical Quarterly* 41 [Fall 1982]: 210).

Chapter 3: Philadelphia, Pa., Princeton, N.J.

1. See Paul Venable Turner, *Campus: An American Planning Tradition* (Cambridge, Mass., 1984), especially chaps. 5 and 6, "The University as City Beautiful" and "The Monastic Quadrangle and Collegiate Ideals." Although Turner does not mention Southwestern, *Campus* is an excellent overall treatment of the development of the American college campus and its architecture. The development of the Gothic Revival in America is a complex subject—a book-length digression to be sure. However, the term *Collegiate Gothic* is used in this study to denote the style that Marcus Whiffen calls "Late Gothic Revival" (*American Architecture Since 1790* [Cambridge, Mass., 1969], pp. 173–77). Whiffen's classification includes ecclesiastical and commercial, as well as educational, architecture, which he labels "Collegiate Gothic." Buildings of the period (roughly 1890 to 1930) by architects such as Ralph Adams Cram, James Gamble Rogers, and Day & Klauder at colleges like Yale, Princeton, and Duke are often termed "eclectic," grouping them with other turn-of-the-century revivalist styles. Certainly the Collegiate Gothic at Southwestern is somewhat "academic," and some historians contend that such work is not as "creative" as, say, the contemporaneous work of Eliel Saarinen at Cranbrook. For example, the National Trust for Historic Preservation's 1983 guide to American architecture, *What Style Is It?,* states: "Reacting to the excesses of High Victorian Gothic, late 19th-century architects returned to a more imitative

Gothic Revival," while the only mention of the Collegiate Gothic notes that the style shaped Princeton and the University of Pennsylvania and "was popular in this period" (p. 41). But the best "eclectic" architects—Cram, Charles McKim, Charles Platt, as well as Southwestern's Charles Klauder—used their chosen style as a starting point, as a discipline that actually encouraged considerable invention.

2. Ralph Adams Cram, "Good and Bad Modern Gothic," *Architectural Review,* August 1899, pp. 117–18. Henry Vaughan's architecture is the subject of a monograph, *The Almighty Wall,* published by the Architectural History Foundation in 1983.

3. Given their pivotal role in the development of the Collegiate Gothic, the literature on Cope & Stewardson is regrettably sparse, but the major sources are: William Emlyn Stewardson, "Cope and Stewardson, The Architects of a Philadelphia Renaissance" (unpublished thesis, Princeton University, 1960); and Cram, "The Work of Messrs. Cope and Stewardson," *Architectural Record,* November 1904, pp. 407–38.

4. Holder Hall was given by Mrs. Russell Sage in honor of a Quaker forebear, which is something of an irony given the dormitory complex's unabashed Anglicanism. Day was the subject of an unpublished doctoral dissertation: Patricia Heintzelman Keebler, "The Life and Work of Frank Miles Day," University of Delaware, 1980. Day was elected president of the American Institute of Architects (AIA) in 1906 and served two terms; he was also a founder of *House and Garden* (1901). "During this period [construction of Holder, 1909 and following] it is evident from general correspondence of the firm that Klauder took an increasing role in its operations as he moved toward partnership . . . . All of the sketches were executed by Klauder"; "Regardless of the difference in stylistic preference between the two men, the association with Klauder was a good one. Together they formed a balance of integrity, creativity, and practicality that made Day and Klauder one of the major architectural firms in the country. Their combined talents were perfectly suited to the needs of institutions with irregular funding and practical functions" (Keebler, "Life and Work," pp. 243–44, 265). Day was largely responsible for Bodley's elevation to honorary membership in the AIA in 1905. Fellow Philadelphia architect John Harbeson contributed the article on Klauder to the *Dictionary of American Biography* (vol. 22, 1944); John Boyer is writing a dissertation at Princeton University on Klauder, "Collegiate Gothic: University Architecture and Medievalism in America, 1885–1916"; see also Sandra Tatman and Roger W. Moss, *Biographical Dictionary of Philadelphia Architects 1700–1930* (Boston, 1985), a Philadelphia Athenaeum reference book that is a good source of information on the entire Philadelphia group of architects. Day & Klauder received the gold medal of the Philadelphia Chapter of the AIA for Holder in 1918, and Klauder received the AIA's gold medal three years later. Day died in 1918, Klauder in 1938.

5. Diehl was carefully covering all his bases in attempting to protect his dream: ". . . and because of their outstanding ability and their familiarity with local conditions, we secured the firm of Jones & Furbringer as supervising architects" ("Ideals," p. 11). The earliest surviving renderings of a college building, those for Palmer Hall, are dated 12 February 1923 and carry the following acknowledgments: H. C. Hibbs, architect; Day and Klauder, Philadelphia, consulting architects; and Jones and Furbringer, Memphis, supervising architects. Also, Southwestern is subtitled with its erstwhile name, "The College of the Mississippi Valley." Curiously, this latter name never took hold, even though "there is one thing upon which President Diehl insists, and that is the correct name of the college of which he is president. Realizing his intense feelings upon this subject two members of the faculty have affectionately dedicated a song to him which is reproduced below. The tune is that of the beautiful old hymn *Autumn.*

We are just plain old Southwestern,
College of the Mississippi Valley;
We are not Southwestern College,
Nor are we Southwestern U,
We are not Southwestern P.U.,
Discriminating are we;
We are just plain old Southwestern,
College of the Mississippi Valley."

(*Southwestern Alumni Magazine* 2 [December 1929]: 7). The "P.U." in the song stood for Presbyterian University, and the college carried that name until 1924; generally called Southwestern, or Southwestern at Memphis, the name officially became Southwestern At Memphis in 1945.

6. Diehl, "Moving a College," p. 15.

7. "Henry C. Hibbs, Architect," *Southern Architect and Building News* 54 (September 1928): 35. In 1932 Southwestern conferred an honorary Master of Fine Arts on Hibbs; *Southwestern Alumni Magazine* (4 [June 1932]: 4) noted his gold medal for Scarritt College Chapel and the "Gold Medal for Southwestern in Educational Architecture, 1929." Despite Hibbs's exposure to the Philadelphia Gothicists, the guiding influence at the University of Pennsylvania in the early years of the century was Paul Philippe Cret (1876–1945). The Beaux Arts–trained Cret taught at Penn until 1907, and as architect Roy Carroll, a fellow student of Hibbs's successor Clinton Parrent, notes, "Charles Klauder never taught at Penn. Our mentor, and the maker of the school was Paul P. Cret—so the classical traditions governed" (Carroll, letter to author, 10 November 1987). In 1933 Cret and Hibbs submitted a competition design for the Davidson County Courthouse in Nashville and won second prize. Nashville architect W. Terrill Hall remembers his father-in-law Henry Hibbs as "a genius, a deep thinker," as well as "an avid fisherman and avid grower of iris." Hall affectionately describes Hibbs as "five feet tall and five feet wide, with little stocky fingers—but boy could he draw!" (Hall, telephone interview with author, 19 April 1988).

8. "Moving a College," p. 16. "Cecil Rhodes did a great thing when he established Rhodes Scholarships in this country, Canada, and Germany. We felt that the men who were appointed to select Rhodes Scholars from the various states were well qualified to make these selections, and we also felt that the colleges of Oxford and Cambridge offered superior advantages. We, therefore, were interested in getting Oxford men as members of our faculty."

9. "Ideals," p. 11.

10. "Ideals," pp. 9–10. Diehl might have also remembered that it was a battle over the placement

and shape of quads at Princeton that effectively forced Woodrow Wilson from the university presidency. Andrew Fleming West, Wilson's adversary, argued for the enclosed quadrangle for the proposed Graduate College rather than the more open plan advocated by Wilson (and for which Cope & Stewardson prepared drawings). As West noted, "Quadrangles enclosing sunny lawns, towers and gateways opening into quiet retreats, ivy-grown walls . . . . These are . . . the answers in architecture and scenic setting to the immemorial longings of academic generations . . . . The exquisite collegiate Gothic found at its best in Oxford and Cambridge . . . fully accords with our desires for Princeton" (*The Graduate College of Princeton* [Princeton, 1913], p. 30).

11. "Ideals," p. 13.

12. Diehl's insistence on maintaining the integrity and high standards of the college revealed itself in the smallest details; during the lean years of the early 1930s, he continued to use engraved calling cards, believing that less expensive printed ones were inappropriate and would give a bad impression.

13. Steve Howard, "The Director as Planner: A Profile of Rhodes College," *Facilities Manager* 2 (Spring 1986): 7.

14. "Ideals," p. 11. In 1931 Diehl was tried for heresy, one charge being the "sheer extravagance" he supposedly lavished on the building of Southwestern. In part of his reply, he said, "We believe there is no future for any denominational college that is not standard or first-class, and the Church must decide whether it will pay the price, or whether it prefers that its colleges go into other hands. There is such a thing as cheap higher education but there is no such thing as good higher education (that is, education that is adequate, honest and Christian) that is cheap" (Cooper, *Southwestern*, p. 129). The charges were brought by eleven Presbyterian ministers of Memphis who accused Diehl of "unsound theological views, mismanagement of the college financial affairs, and the loss of confidence on the part of the Presbyterian constituency in Memphis in his administration." The Board of Directors, meeting on 3 February 1931, vindicated Dr. Diehl and also offered an official appreciation, part of which read: "Is there another man within the four Synods who could have accomplished what Dr. Diehl has done? It took manliness, it took courage, it took faith, it took persistency, it took industry, it took brain with artistic ability and business acumen, it took heart devoted to Christ, our Lord, to build, to equip and pay for Southwestern as it stands today, and that with opposition without and at times within" (*Southwestern Alumni Magazine* 3 [February-March 1931]: 13, 10).

15. "Ideals," p. 7.

16. "Moving a College," p. 12. On the drawings of February and March 1923, Palmer is simply labeled "Administration Building."

17. In 1968 the Science Hall was rededicated in honor of Berthold S. Kennedy of the class of 1912, who gave $300,000 for its renovation; its construction cost in 1924–1925 was $350,000.

18. "Ideals," pp. 11–12. The drawings for Robb, Calvin, and a third dormitory were dated 22 September 1923 and were revised 14 April 1924; they are titled "Men's Dormitories Numbers 1–2–3." The Southwestern dorms are really quite straightforward in plan and basic living arrangement (undoubtedly dictated as much by cost as by aesthetic considerations), especially when compared with Cram's Graduate College at Princeton, where the "problem of vitalizing what is mechanical never confronted the designer . . . The variety of its rooms, the lengths, twistings, changes in levels, widths, and heights of its staircases, and the isolation of sets of rooms from other sets are founded in the principles of individuality and sociability. But, also, in this cluttered diversity of changing levels and interminable staircases, there is an open denial of the worth of efficiency" (Albert Bush-Brown, "Cram and Gropius: Traditionalism and Progressivism," *New England Quarterly*, March 1952, 20). Bush-Brown's article compares the Graduate College at Princeton with the International-style Graduate Center at Harvard by Walter Gropius—one of the icons of Modernism in America. The factory-like Cambridge complex of 1950 was universally hailed as an antidote to places like Princeton, Duke, and Southwestern. As Gropius told the Harvard alumni, "How can we expect our students to become bold and fearless in thought and action if we encase them in sentimental shrines feigning a culture which has long since disappeared?" (ibid., p. 4). Gropius's brave new world of educational architecture was conceived on the principle that students should not be burdened with irrelevant historical facts or surrounded by buildings "sentimentally copied from by-gone periods" (p. 14). While there is merit in Gropius's ideas of reforming society through architecture—and the post–World War I European milieu from which he emerged had indeed seemed to demand a rejection of the historical styles revived in the late nineteenth century—his Harvard housing is no more morally superior or intrinsically better than the traditional Oxbridge dormitories at Princeton and Southwestern. Admittedly, Cram's Graduate College is amusing when viewed as the national memorial to Grover Cleveland, designed for a Presbyterian school by the son of a Unitarian minister, in the style of Cardinal Wolsey's Oxford.

19. In his dedicatory remarks of 13 November 1947, Diehl noted of White, "He was generous to a fault and entertained a wide circle of friends in a manner befitting a man of wisdom, modesty and refinement. He was a man whose word was his bond and whose physical appearance was as superb as his mind was outstanding. Upon Gordon White's death nearly thirty-one years ago the late Justice McReynolds, of the Tennessee Supreme Court, said, 'Gordon was an Apollo in life, he is a god in death.' "

20. Cram, "Cope and Stewardson," p. 423. Although it has an unfortunate ring to contemporary ears, Cram used the word *racial* to mean Anglo-Saxon, or Anglo-American. Nevertheless, when reading Cram today one may detect a certain snobbery, elitism, and perhaps even racism in his thinking. Yet Cram's ethnocentricity is not so unusual when seen in the context of its own day, against the background of, say, the Imperial vision of Cecil Rhodes and Theodore Roosevelt, the writing of Kipling or the marches of Elgar, or even the Anglophilia of Woodrow Wilson. The "American Ruskin," Cram wrote two dozen books and scores of articles, and his position in American cultural history is not easily distilled into a footnote.

21. Diehl, "Southwestern College, Memphis, Tenn.," *Southern Architect and Building News* 54

(September 1928): 66. Although a presidential residence was part of the original master plan, the Diehls lived in the south end of Neely Hall. In 1956 Southwestern purchased a stone and half-timbered house at 671 West Drive in Hein Park as the president's residence. *Southwestern News* (19 [December 1956]: 1) described it as "a beautiful stone house so appropriately designed and located as to seem a part of the original college plan . . . of English design."

22. Larson's book was coauthored by Archie MacInnes Palmer and published by the American Association of Colleges, an organization which Diehl would later serve as president—and which James Daughdrill would later chair. Larson's book may be seen as a sort of competitor to Klauder's *College Architecture*. Larson, as confirmed a Georgian as Diehl et al. were Gothicists, did extensive "Collegiate Colonial" work at Dartmouth, Louisville, the Institute for Advanced Study (a near neighbor to Cram's Graduate College at Princeton), and other schools, including entire new campuses for Colby in Waterville, Maine, and for Wake Forest in Winston-Salem, North Carolina.

23. "Why the Lynx? A History," *The Sou'wester,* 28 April 1978, p. 4. Diehl liked the analogy that both the lynx and Southwestern were small but tenacious, and he believed that his was the only school with that particular mascot.

Chapter 4: The Colossus of Dr. Rhodes

1. "The exterior of the building will match Palmer Hall in appearance except that the stones and rubble stones and the slate roof will be of very thin lines, giving the entire building a feeling of femininity . . . . The entire building is to be reinforced with concrete and fireproofed. In the asphalt-tile floors there will be cinder blocks which will prevent the transmission of sound from one floor to another. All walls will have a four foot plaster wainscot above which there will be an exposed acoustic cinder block, painted in tints to match the walls . . . . Two fireplaces, one in each wing, will make it possible to have log fires on cold winter nights" ("Women's Dormitory Well Under Way," *Southwestern News* 8 [March 1946]: 6).

2. Voorhies cost $425,000, Ellett $165,000. The construction is also not medieval. Ellett is the "very latest word in men's dorms, it is as fireproof as any modern building can possibly be, with only doors and a few window sills constructed of wood. All doorframes, baseboards, and moldings are of enameled steel; the outside walls are of stone and the interior is of steel and concrete, well sealed against dampness and rodents; even the floors are asphalt laid on concrete. Huge brass doors, built to last forever, grace the five entrances—sound protection against 'absolutely anything—storm, cold, or dampness,' and each suite has two complete sets of matching maple furniture" (*Southwestern News* 9 [May 1947]: 2).

3. The donor of the library specified that the architect had to be "local." According to Mary Williamson Parrent, widow of architect Clinton Parrent, Southwestern never made any plans in the event of Henry Hibbs's death (interview with author, 11 October 1987). Although it may never be known exactly which designer was most responsible for the actual design of Voorhies and Ellett, perhaps it would be fair to say that those dormitories were the work of both Hibbs and Parrent.

4. "Pres.-Emeritus Diehl's Statement," *Southwestern News* 12 (August 1950): 2. Echoing Diehl's sentiments, Mrs. Andrew Dale of Columbia, Tennessee, a supporter of the college, noted, "It is said that education and character are two things that cannot be taken from you. In Christian education you get both together. This is a magnificent gift to Christian education" (*Memphis Press-Scimitar,* 28 June 1950, editorial page).

5. *The Commercial Appeal,* 2 March 1952, sec. 1, p. 14.

6. "Need for New Building Explained by Librarian," *Southwestern News* 12 (August 1950): 4.

7. "Mr. and Mrs. A. K. Burrow Give $600,000 Library to S'western," *Southwestern News* 12 (August 1950): 1. There are two renderings by Walk C. Jones, Jr., for five faculty houses—one group is Gothic (similar to the fraternities), the other is Colonial Revival. These probably date from the mid-1920s and were envisioned for the northeast corner of the campus, but never got beyond the idea stage.

8. Roper, *Southwestern,* pp. 18–19. The masons at Burrow did not, contrary to usual Southwestern construction, vary the dimensions and thickness of the roof slates (see Helen Watkins Norman, "Carved in Stone," *Rhodes College Today* 2 [28 February 1985]: 10).

9. James E. Roper, "Southwestern at Memphis, 1848–1981," *Tennessee Historical Quarterly* 41 (Fall 1982): 216.

10. In response to a request for a biography from Max Killeen, editor of the *Journal of Southern Architecture* in Baton Rouge, Parrent listed the libraries at Fisk, Tulsa, South Carolina, and Davidson as his designs (copy of letter, Parrent to Killeen, 9 July 1959, collection of Mary W. Parrent, Nashville, Tenn.)

11. For biographical information on Parrent, see obituaries in *Nashville Banner,* 2 October 1967, and *Nashville Tennessean,* 1 October 1967; Parrent gets a brief mention in Joseph L. Herndon, "Architects in Tennessee until 1930: A Dictionary" (Master's thesis, Columbia University, 1975), p. 145. Of his student days and training at the University of Pennsylvania, classmate and later associate Roy Carroll offered the following: "I have no special ideas as to Clint Parrent's 'Gothic' work. He probably followed Hibbs . . . and the documents . . . . I am not at all sure Clint ever was in Cret's atelier, but we all studied the various historical styles" (letter to author, 18 December 1987).

12. Mary Parrent, interview with author, 11 October 1987. Parrent's office files contain a number of letters from grateful debtors, usually friends to whom he had loaned money. Parrent gave generously to church and charities, including Southwestern. Henry Hibbs had also served as president of the Tennessee AIA.

13. *Domestic Architecture of England* was purchased from Carl Wendelin Kuehny in Cleveland for sixty-five dollars in August 1952; one of the authors, Thomas Garner, had been a partner of Henry Vaughan's mentor, George Frederick Bodley. In 1966 Parrent ordered Christian Norberg-Schulz's contro-

versial *Intentions in Architecture,* suggesting that he tried to keep abreast with the literature of his profession. Parrent intended to leave his architectural library to Southwestern.

14. Louise Davis, "Stripped to the Buff: Tennessee's State Library Makes a Hit," *Nashville Tennessean Magazine,* 8 February 1953, 6–9. Parrent reviewed Agnes Addison Gilchrist's *William Strickland, Architect and Engineer, 1788–1854* for the *Tennessee Historical Quarterly* (10 [1951]: 91–92), which included the following: "From the viewpoint of an architect, I would have preferred for Mrs. Gilchrist to have included many more floor plans and construction details for, after all, the exterior style is like a suit of clothes which does not tell you very much of the inner man."

15. Parrent, "Adolphus Heiman and the Building Methods of Two Centuries," *Tennessee Historical Quarterly* 12 (1953): 207, 209–10. The last line of the quotation was borrowed (with acknowledgment) from Talbot Hamlin, *Forms and Functions of Twentieth Century Architecture.*

16. Diehl, "Moving a College," p. 12. Ground for the gymnasium was broken in January 1953, construction was completed in June 1954, and the dedication was in December 1954.

17. "Ceremony to Start Memorial for Hero," *The Commercial Appeal,* 4 January 1953, front page and seq. This article also includes part of a poem by H. I. Phillips, a columnist for the *New York Sun,* which began:

"The man who did the most . . ."
How routine did it seem
In those bright college years,
Now something of a dream.
"The man who did the most . . ."
How true those words of yore
As "Memphis Bill" checks out—
To "hit the line" no more!

18. "Original plans included a women's gym and a swimming pool at the east end of the structure, the whole being estimated at $900,000. Necessity, however, limited the actuality to the estimated $623,000 which would build only the main gym" (Roper, *Southwestern,* p. 24). The 136- by 60-foot addition, dedicated 17 March 1971 as the Ruth Sherman Hyde Memorial Gym for Women, was designed by Barge, Waggoner and Sumner of Nashville. In a letter to Mary Parrent (17 January 1970), Peyton Rhodes wrote, "The other day we signed a contract (without the money all in sight) to complete the women's part of the gym at last . . . . We are making the exterior exactly as originally planned." The actual designer of Hyde was Thomas Woodard, who entered the architectural profession as an apprentice to Clinton Parrent in 1949. "It was my pleasure to work on the design of several buildings at Southwestern with Mr. Parrent. Among them were the old Refectory, Infirmary, Mallory Gymnasium, Freshman Girls Dormitory, and my favorite, Halliburton Memorial Tower. Any drawings that are marked TW were prepared by me. I made preliminary studies for the proportion of the Tower and made full size cut stone drawings for the project . . . . I left Mr. Parrent's office in 1963 and joined the firm of Barge, Waggoner, Sumner and Cannon in 1965. During my years with Mr. Parrent, I established a close personal relationship with Dr. Peyton Rhodes. After Mr. Parrent's death, Dr. Rhodes contacted me to design the addition to Mallory Gymnasium. The design followed the basic 1953 design of Hyde Women's Gym with modifications dictated by the change in program during the interim period. My knowledge of the Gothic Style was a result of my apprenticeship with Mr. Parrent" (letter to author, 10 February 1988). In 1977 the swimming pool was realized through the gift of Bob and Emily Alburty; Mr. Alburty founded Business Service Industries, which developed the office background music known as Muzak; the pool was the work of Robert Browne, architect of Austin Hall.

19. Mallory looks not unlike the medieval work of Sir Edwin Lutyens, say, the English architect's Castle Drogo in Devon, 1910–1930, or his restoration of Lindisfarne Castle, Northumberland, of 1903.

20. Ten years later, following a visit to the campus, Kevin Lynch, the renowned planner from MIT, wrote President Rhodes about the dissolution of the original quad plan (17 April 1963). As a modernist, Lynch freely admitted that he did not approve of Southwestern's continued use of what he regarded as an "eclectic" style. But he greatly admired the cohesiveness and unity of the Gothic-inspired quadrangles; he warned against the danger of allowing "isolated structures" and advised Rhodes to keep the buildings connected.

21. The Hibbs office did six pencil elevations and a section of Townsend, dated 6 August 1945. Townsend cost $315,000.

22. Roper, *Southwestern,* p. 26.

23. Parrent, "Adolphus Heiman," pp. 210–11.

24. Ibid., p. 212.

25. Ibid., p. 211.

26. The bell was cast by Paccard Frères according to specifications prepared by Arthur L. Bigelow, the bell master at Princeton. "Mr. Halliburton was looking for a particular bell tone that he remembered from his boyhood and Mr. Bigelow's description of 'the living, pulsating, swirling tones of a deep-throated bronze' was a perfect description of what he remembered" (Parrent, "To Build a Tower," typescript, p. 14).

27. Letter, Halliburton to Parrent, 14 April 1963. Halliburton also expressed his pleasure "over the evidence of good will and friendly cooperation felt by all who had a part in this enterprise, from the hod carriers up to the one with the high appreciation of form and beauty who conceived it." The letter is signed "Your friend and admirer." The tower is only one part of an expansion to the west and north of Palmer called Gooch Hall, which extends 90 feet to the rear of the tower and provided an additional 11,200 square feet of space (the tower has some 3,800 square feet); this four-story administrative annex was called the Tower Building until 1981.

28. This and subsequent quotations about the Kellogg Center are from notes made by Peyton Rhodes on 21 March 1970 and titled "Kellogg-Continuing Education Center—H. Clinton Parrent, following meeting of Executive Committee of Board on Feb. 16, 1970."

29. Letter from Emory W. Morris, president, Kellogg Foundation, to Peyton Rhodes, 19 November 1963. In a letter written to Parrent the following

week (26 November 1963), Rhodes expressed his dismay at the turn of events. What was particularly galling was that while Southwestern did not "know why Kellogg reversed completely every indication of acceding to our proposal . . . , they turned around immediately and gave $1,000,000, which is the amount we were asking, to Notre Dame, which institution had no work at all in continuing education" (Rhodes, "Kellogg-Continuing Education Center").

30. "It might be asked why there was not a written contract with the Architect about the proposed structure. Since first Hibbs and Parrent, and then Parrent had been architects from the building of the college as it began about 1923, and since we never failed to build anything that there was a clear need for and which had been developed, both the architect and the college had worked along in a fairly informal manner over the years in the construction of any project" (Rhodes, "Kellogg-Continuing Education"). Or, as Mary Parrent confirmed, "It was all on good faith" (interview with author, 10 October 1987). Mr. Parrent's bill of $22,693.50 for the Kellogg Center was accompanied by the architect's willingness to carry "the Center for Continuing Education on our books until such time as Southwestern finds a donor" (Parrent to C. L. Springfield, comptroller of Southwestern, 18 November 1965), yet that amount covered supplies and payment for draftsmen (and the hiring of Schell Lewis, whom Rhodes called "the foremost renderer in America," to prepare a rendering to send to the Kellogg Foundation). Four years after the Kellogg project fell through, Parrent wrote Springfield again: "If Southwestern has abandoned the Adult Center there is a formula in the A.I.A. contract for handling abandoned projects, see Art. 8.4. I cannot afford to make such a large donation to Southwestern under the present circumstances" (Parrent to Springfield, 15 September 1967). Parrent did indeed contribute to Southwestern over the years and also "gave" more through patience in waiting on payment, keeping his fees low, and by not billing the college "for any of the campus plans" (Parrent to Springfield, 18 November 1965). In the Kellogg-Parrent memorandum, Rhodes concluded by saying, "It is my opinion that we owe Mr. Parrent's estate a payment for his work," and accordingly Southwestern settled with the architect's widow. In a memorandum to Springfield on the same matter, Rhodes said of the preliminary plans, "They are good ones and as sound now as they were in 1963–64" (15 March 1967).

31. *Sou'wester,* 1 April 1965. There was also a face of Diehl mounted on Glassell at the same time, but it was lost after its removal; the Rhodes gargoyle, saved by the staff of Physical Plant, reappeared as part of the wall of the new "East" dormitory twenty years later. The "stonecutter" was actually Wayne Christy, owner of Christy Cut Stone.

32. Roper, *Southwestern,* , p. 46.

33. Ibid. As constructed, the Student Center was little changed in configuration from an architect's drawing (Fig. 67) published in *Southwestern News,* March 1945, p. 6, although this Hibbs-Parrent design is for a far larger building.

34. Roper, "Southwestern at Memphis, 1848–1981," p. 219. The Ford Foundation's challenge grant was part of its Special Program in Education, "the objective of which is to advance the development of selected private institutions of higher education as *national and regional centers of excellence*." Part of the cost of the Science Center was paid for with federal monies, and their use put a number of constraints on the design.

35. Carroll had recently completed a term as president of the AIA, and his firm, Carroll, Grisdale & VanAlen, Architects, had done considerable collegiate work at Penn, Temple, Haverford, Swarthmore, and other schools, albeit in a distinctly Modernist vein. The agreement with Carroll, Grisdale & Van Alen of Philadelphia to "associate as architects" was signed 15 July 1965. Two months earlier, Parrent had written to Joseph Richardson, a principal in the respected Boston firm of Shepley, Bulfinch, Richardson, & Abbott: "Would you consider any form of association with me to do this Science Center?" (4 May 1965, copy, Parrent office files); Parrent also told Richardson "Southwestern is one of the very best of my clients." Richardson replied that he had to decline because of too many projects at Harvard and elsewhere, but left open the possibility of future collaboration (7 May 1965). Carroll's firm also designed the international terminal at Philadelphia Airport, NASA headquarters in Washington (with Holabird & Root), and the offices of Campbell Soup Company in Henry Hibbs's hometown of Camden, New Jersey.

36. "I cannot recall whether or not Clint knew we had designed a large library, about 75 percent of which was underground. My partner Jack Grisdale and I decided to build most of the Science Center underground to preserve the openness of that part of the Campus, and build as little Gothic-like structures as possible in the same area" (Carroll to author, 25 October 1987).

37. A remodeling of Kennedy Hall into the Department of Chemistry was also part of the Science Center; however, as Mr. Parrent lamented in a letter to Lomax Springfield, "I was replaced by Mr. Henry Donnelly . . . . It seems that my work has not been appreciated" (15 September 1967). Parrent had done some of the work on Kennedy, and his letter to Springfield is to inquire about his unpaid bill for $970.24, as well as to ask once again for payment for his firm's work on the Kellogg Center. Donnelly was an engineer.

Chapter 5: Dr. Daughdrill's Chariot of Fire

1. The college has blueprints dated 24 April 1968; the dorm opened April 1969. It was rededicated in 1980 in honor of Anne Marie Caskey Williford, who was dean of women and subsequently dean of students at the time of her death in 1979 at age forty-nine.

2. Alice Fulbright, "Southwestern's Clough Hall Is Result of Sibling Affection," *Commercial Appeal,* 14 October 1970, p. 20. Mr. Clough was chairman of the board of Abbott Laboratories. Another contributor was Mrs. Ailsa Mellon Bruce, who gave one hundred thousand dollars anonymously before her death.

3. Peyton Rhodes, letter to Mary Parrent, 17 January 1970. "The building was carefully planned to perpetuate the whole architectural scheme of the campus, although as a sophisticated, thoroughly modern building, it actually represents a considerable departure from older buildings" (*Southwestern*

News 34 [December 1970]: 7–8). Wells Awsumb recalls Clough Hall: "It was a difficult job, arranging five disparate departments in a pseudo-gothic structure which had to look good as well. Fitting it into the east side of campus, creating and organizing the quadrangle with focal point and connections to other buildings, arranging the main lobby as actually a see-through and pass-through to the buildings being cut off by Clough was a challenge. There could be no front and back; both east and west elevations must be impressive, then the 'services' at several points and cooling tower and other back door items must be obviated (the cooling tower went to the roof in a low tower); service was located at several points nearest their final use area" (letter to author, 24 January 1988). Mr. Awsumb was subsequently commissioned to prepare designs for an auditorium. "This building was to accommodate the entire student body, be suitable for music and theatre together with all necessary support spaces. Also house a new dining hall. Some of these requirements were impractical in one hall where really three different audiences would use it. We went as far as schematic drawings and a rendering, but as I remember it all became too expensive so we renovated the existing food service and kitchen and began a design for a theatre. We had just completed the very successful Theatre Memphis so we (along with our consultant) were well qualified to do a good job. About the time we had completed the preliminary design the board decided they needed to hear from several architects and the result was that we did not get the job" (ibid.). One might infer that Southwestern was displeased or disappointed with the architect's designs, but the auditorium really was not needed and would not have been used often enough to justify its cost. Wells Awsumb was subsequently authorized to prepare a preliminary study for a theatre. Although presented to the Board, the project languished, presumably for lack of funding; a drama building was finally realized with the renovation of Zeta Tau Alpha in 1981.

4. The early 1970s was a fallow period for building at Southwestern, with only the construction of the Hyde Women's Gymnasium during what Roper calls "the brief and ascetic Bowden regime" (Roper's chapter in *Southwestern* on Bowden's presidency is titled "After Christmas Comes a Lent").

5. Metcalf Crump, interview with author, 2 December 1987. "I was involved in developing master planning studies for President Daughdrill in 1981 in order to find a proper site for Hassell Hall. My selection and recommendation of the Hassell Hall site was in part an effort to weave together the unraveled fabric of the northeast corner of the campus. The siting of Hassell Hall served to anchor a new quadrangle to the south of the buildings as well as to the north. TAC confirmed this concept in their 1986 Master Plan. Since 1981, I have continued to provide the college, periodically, with Master Planning Studies. These included the studies which I prepared during the programming and planning of East Residence Hall and the New Dormitory which I sited prior to the 1986 TAC Master Plan. Last summer, I was asked by President Daughdrill to prepare a completely computerized Existing Campus Plan as well as to develop concept studies incorporating my own views with regard to future growth on the Rhodes College campus . . . . My first project at Rhodes College was the complete interior renovation of Robb, White, Ellett, and Bellingrath Dormitories in 1979. The scope of the renovation included the removal of all radiators and window air conditioning units as well as the demolition of a number of walls and partitions. New suites and room configurations were designed and built in some areas and a complete new heating, ventilating, and air conditioning system was installed. The engineers retained by Rhodes College planned to install a large above-ground air conditioning chiller in the middle of the dormitory courtyard. I argued vehemently and successfully to spend the extra funds to submerge this equipment in a well and cover it with a grille. This decision prevented what surely would have been an enormous eyesore in the center of what is one of the most handsome quadrangular spaces on the campus. A more recent renovation project was the extensive renovation of Burrow library. The most visible results are the new dark paneling, lighting, cabinetry, carpet, and finishes in the main entrance lobby, circulation desk area, reading room, reference room, and periodicals areas. This work was begun in the summer of 1986 and completed in August 1988. Other recent projects include the stone base of the lynx sculpture near Rhodes Tower and two separate studies on exterior and interior graphics and signage throughout the campus" (Crump, letter to author, 4 January 1989).

6. Exactly a year after the trustees' resolution the college appointed E. Dudley Howe as director of Physical Plant. Dudley Howe came to the newly named Rhodes College with experience as both an architect and a hospital administrator (he has a degree in business administration from Ohio State; he served a four-year apprenticeship with Frank Lloyd Wright; and as a member of the Taliesin Fellowship, Howe worked on two of Wright's last projects, Beth Sholom Synagogue outside Philadelphia and the Guggenheim Museum in New York). In 1989 Howe became director of Physical Plant at Stetson University.

7. Crump's work is perhaps analogous to that of English architect Quinlan Terry (b. 1937), a controversial designer whose "Eighteenth Century Classical Revival" buildings reflect a belief that "the revolution started by the Modern Movement has been completed . . . . The Modern Movement set the world on its head. We are now standing on our feet again. It is as though the Modern Movement had not happened" (Clive Aslet, *Quinlan Terry* [New York, 1986], p. 209). While Crump is not limited to one style, nor is he as dogmatic, Aslet's assessment of Terry's New Howard Building at Downing College, Cambridge (1983–1986), might serve for East and New Halls as well: ". . . it is more a piece of pure architecture, where the object in view is a beautiful building, than a hard profit and loss calculation. It also stands as a happy, if rare, emblem of the way in which academic learning can be of practical benefit to both the world at large and the college in particular" (p. 202). Downing College might make an interesting comparison with Rhodes. Founded in 1800 (the first new Cambridge college in over two hundred years), Downing attracted wide public attention when it was built in the Greek Revival style, and the college has continued to erect classical buildings right down to Terry's work. "These have been choices dictated not simply by considerations

of what was fashionable at any given time, but rather by some surprisingly strong, collective architectural taste which has dared, again and again, to go against the prevailing tide. This consistency makes the architecture of Downing a remarkable monument to two centuries of classicism, unparalleled anywhere else in the world" (bookseller's promotional brochure for Cinzia Maria Sicca, *Committed to Classicism: The Building of Down College, Cambridge*, published by Downing College, 1987).

8. " 'The iron oxide is what gives Rhodes' stone its range of reds, yellows and browns,' said Metcalf Crump . . . . One doesn't find those colors in the stone at other institutions . . . . 'Rhodes' stone is fairly unique.' The variegated look of the stonework also comes from 'sculptings,' slices of red and green slate which are fitted into the sandstone patchwork. East Hall, for instance, will have about one part slate to twenty parts sandstone. 'Eyebrows,' pieces of slate or stone that project from the face of the wall, add texture and definition. It takes approximately 540 tons of stone and a half-dozen or so stone masons working three or four months to raise the walls of a dormitory the size of East Hall. . . . Gerald McKenzie, a twelfth generation stone mason who is supervising the East Hall work, says he must move his masons around three or four times a day. Such maneuvering maintains the 'random' look of Rhodes' stonework . . . . 'There are so many variations in the detailing of the buildings . . . more possibilities than you might find in modern architecture,' said Met Crump" (Norman, "Carved in Stone," *Rhodes College Today*, p. 10).

9. The new dining hall, called Refectory West Hall, was the recipient of a 1988 Excellence in Masonry Architectural Award. Citing both design and the use of masonry, the judges for the Masonry Institute of Tennessee noted the rarity of a new building that has "masonry and craftsmanship worthy of its historical precedent."

10. TAC is located in Cambridge, Massachusetts, while the SOM branch involved at Rhodes was the Houston office. The other firms considered were Richard Dober (Belmont, Mass.), Edward Pinckney (Hilton Head, S.C.), Perry Dean Rogers (Boston), H2L2 (Philadelphia), Richter Cornbrooks, Gribble (Baltimore), Burgess & Niple (Columbus, Ohio), Architects Design Collaborative (Kansas City), and Johnson, Johnson & Roy (Ann Arbor, Mich.). "All the firms on this list are credible and have worked on campus master plans for some of the most prestigious colleges and universities around the Country . . . . My first choice was Dick Dober. I like Dick's style, his method of approach and the very personal attention he gives to every project. Dick called several days after receiving information that he was in the final selection and withdrew his name due to prior commitments . . . . Early in our selection process we decided we wanted someone from outside our area who was unfamiliar with Rhodes and Memphis and would give us a fresh perspective of what they envisioned Rhodes to be in the future . . . . The one person who most readily grasped the feeling and appearance we wanted to accomplish was Mr. Shep Williams, Landscape Architect with TAC. Shep has a feeling for nature, for landscape, for the natural material we use and the importance of a humanistic bond of all these factors. He was able to project this in very realistic terms and with specificity. He did not lose sight of the fact that we are a very busy college and that all normal functions must continue on a daily basis. It was probably Shep Williams who sold TAC to the interview and selection committee" (Dudley Howe, letter to author, 4 February 1988).

11. Initially, the Master Plan called for a new refectory to the east of Williford and Trezevant, as well as two dormitories forming a quadrangle with Williford, East, and New Halls. These proposed dorms were to be located on the site of the present sororities, five of which were to be new structures linked together and forming a quad (naturally) with the existing fraternity houses. The board voted to drop this portion of the plan. Spann Place is the first of three phases of University Quadrangle and has five houses (the center part of the complex will have eight houses, the northern segment will have thirteen). Each house is self-contained (there are three bedrooms, two baths, and living and kitchen facilities) so that it can be used for student housing, faculty homes, seminars, rental property, and the like. University Quadrangle was the result of a limited competition, with The Crump Firm, Gassner Nathan & Partners, and the chosen firm of MMH Hall, Architects/Planners. Principals March H. and Mitchell M. Hall are both graduates of Pennsylvania State University; their firm was founded in 1970 (the same year as Crump & Taylor) and has done a variety of design and planning work, including the Alex Haley Museum and Tourist Complex. The five gables that form the Tutwiler Street facade of Spann Place project from a slate roof that has an irregular cornice line, suggesting that the architects failed to grasp the overall linearity of the neighboring Hibbs and Parrent dorms. On the rear is an arcade which, while intriguing visually, is supported by an exposed steel lintel that is totally at odds with the constructional basis of Gothic—the masonry arch. Spann Place is only superficially in keeping with the rest of the campus.

Appendix

1. *Southwestern Alumni Magazine* 2 (May 1930): 22.
2. Ibid., 5 (May-June 1933): 14.
3. Ibid., p. 15.
4. *Southwestern News,* February 1950, p. 5. The estimated cost of the new sorority was sixteen thousand dollars.
5. The minutes of a meeting of the Trustees of the Pi Kappa Alpha Memorial Foundation held in Memphis on 18 March 1949 carry the stipulation that the architect be a member of the fraternity.
6. Notes from the second session of the Supreme Council Meeting of Pi Kappa Alpha held in Washington on 25 November 1949 mention that "since the Evergreen Presbyterian Church is in the process of erecting a red brick sanctuary using the strict Colonial style of architecture, and because of the considerably greater expense of Collegiate Gothic style with stone construction, the Council officially expressed its desire to have the architect prepare plans on the basis of a red brick building in some Colonial style of architecture." Mahoney was hired sometime between this meeting and March 1950.

Index

Credits

The photographs in this volume are reproduced through the courtesy of the following institutions, individuals, and publishers. The numbers refer to figure numbers.

The Crump Firm, 76, 79, 95
Harvard University, 7
Alan Karchmer, 74
Charles Klauder and Herbert C. Wise, *College Architecture in America* (1929), 27
Jens Frederick Larson, *Architectural Planning of the American College* (1933), 15
William Morgan, 8, 22, 33, 73, 91
Mary Parrent, 35, 40, 42, 43, 48, 60, 61, 62, 63, 69
Princeton University Archives, 5, 6, 11, 12, 21, 28
Rhodes College, 1, 2, 4, 16, 17, 18, 19, 23, 24, 25, 26, 29, 30, 31, 32, 34, 36, 37, 38, 39, 41, 44, 45, 46, 47, 50, 51, 52, 53, 54, 55, 56, 57, 58, 59, 64, 65, 66, 67, 68, 70, 71, 72, 75, 77, 78, 80, 82, 83, 84, 85, 86, 87, 88, 89, 90, 92
Murray Riss, 81
St. Paul's School, 9
Southern Architect and Building News, 14
Southwestern Alumni Magazine, 3, 13
Southwestern News, 93, 94
Thomas-Photos, Oxford, 20
Philip Thomason, 49
University of Pittsburgh, University Archives, 10

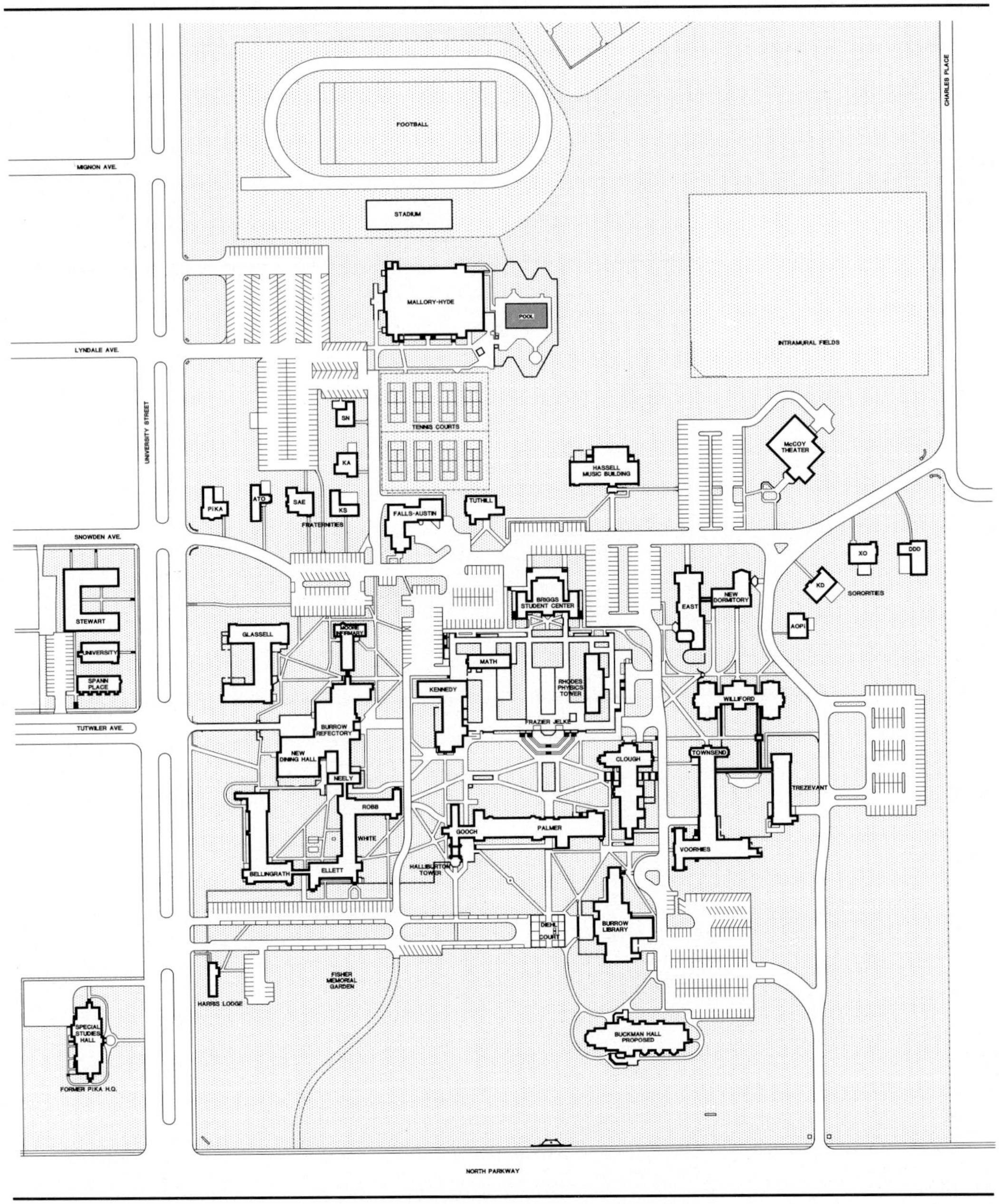

95. Campus map, 1989 (The Crump Firm).